RETURN ON SUSTAINABILITY

How Business Can Increase Profitability
and Address Climate Change
in an Uncertain Economy

Kevin Wilhelm

Foreword by Bob Willard

Vice President, Publisher: Tim Moore
Associate Publisher and Director of Marketing: Amy Neidlinger
Editorial Assistant: Pamela Boland
Operations Specialist: Jodi Kemper
Marketing Manager: Megan Graue
Cover Designer: Chuti Prasertsith
Managing Editor: Kristy Hart
Editor: Kaia Peterson
Manufacturing Buyer: Dan Uhrig

© 2013 by Kevin Wilhelm
Published by Pearson Education, Inc.
Publishing as FT Press
Upper Saddle River, New Jersey 07458

FT Press offers excellent discounts on this book when ordered in quantity for bulk purchases or special sales. For more information, please contact U.S. Corporate and Government Sales, 1-800-382-3419, corpsales@pearsontechgroup.com. For sales outside the U.S., please contact International Sales at international@pearsoned.com.

Company and product names mentioned herein are the trademarks or registered trademarks of their respective owners.

Printed in the United States of America

First Printing May 2013

ISBN-10: 0-13-344550-X
ISBN-13: 978-0-13-344550-3

Pearson Education LTD.
Pearson Education Australia PTY, Limited.
Pearson Education Singapore, Pte. Ltd.
Pearson Education Asia, Ltd.
Pearson Education Canada, Ltd.
Pearson Educación de Mexico, S.A. de C.V.
Pearson Education—Japan
Pearson Education Malaysia, Pte. Ltd.

Library of Congress Control Number: 2013935818

Table of Contents

Acknowledgments

This book could never have been possible without the work and support of my wonderful staff at the time of this writing—Ruth Lee, Anne DeMelle, and Jessie Alan. Throughout the entire process of writing this book, they put in tireless hours of research, writing, and editing to truly make this book what it is today. They challenged my thoughts, tore apart my work, and put up with my chicken-scratch type edits.

To Ruth, who has been with me the whole time at SBC, I am so thankful for everything you've done to not only make this book a success, but our company a success. Thank you for all your last-minute thoughts, help on images, and everything you did to bring this to fruition. It is a pleasure to come to work with you every day. You motivate me to be a better consultant, boss, writer, and person. You are joy to work with, are the absolute best employee and business partner I've ever had, and this company would not be where it is today without you.

I'd like to thank Elisa Pond for her research, Kaia Peterson for her amazing edits and insight, and Bob Willard for serving as a source of motivation for me in my day to day business pursuits.

I'd also like to thank all of my friends, colleagues, and the BGI gang who persuaded me to write this book, but especially Meghan Golden and Mary Rick for their constant encouragement and amazing friendship.

However, above and beyond anyone else, none of this would have been possible without the support and encouragement of the love of my life, my wife, JO. You are my inspiration for this book, and you more than anyone else, are responsible for my passion and commitment to saving the environment. Thank you for your patience during this entire process, for your help and understanding during those long winter nights and weekend afternoons when I stayed home and sequestered myself to the couch to write this book. If not for you and the countless bits of wisdom that you've imparted on me over these past 18 years, I never would be in this field, and I certainly would never have written this book. You are my reason for being, and there is not a more fortunate husband on this planet. I love you.

Foreword

By Bob Willard

The 2007 Intergovernmental Panel on Climate Change (IPCC) reports state that we only have a few years in which to stabilize our greenhouse gases (GHG) before we experience irreversible and precipitous climate change.[i] The Millennium Ecosystem Assessment (MEA) says that 60% of the 24 ecosystems on which we depend are being degraded or used unsustainably, while the rest are in jeopardy.[ii] Humanity's Ecological Footprint is already 23% larger than the planet can sustain, and it is growing.[iii] The United Nations Environment Programme (UNEP) *Global Environment Outlook (GEO-4)* says that major persistent threats to the planet such as climate change, the rate of species extinction, and the challenges of feeding a growing population, to name a few, are all putting humanity at risk.[iv]

These are crises, and they have planet earth teetering on the edge of a tipping point. We are in a race to see if humanity can save the world that nurtures us. Happily, solutions are known and within our capabilities. We do not have a deficiency of solutions, but a deficiency of leadership. We need to stop unsustainable practices that are precipitating this planetary emergency. We need to declare a War on Climate Change to galvanize our collective resolve. This can and needs to be done, even during the uncertainty of our current economic situation.

We can bring the same level of urgency and resources to the climate, energy, and ecological crises as we have to the War on Terror. Governments AND corporations need to take leadership actions to future-proof society. This book succinctly describes benefits that companies can reap from actions motivated by enlightened self-interest, so long as those corporate efforts are focused and supported by the following six bold actions that immediately address the pervasive monumental environmental and social challenges facing us.

1. Support integrating Education for Sustainable Development (ESD) throughout all education systems.

The goal of the United Nations Decade of Education for Sustainable Development,[v] 2005–2014, is to integrate the principles, values, and practices of sustainable development into all aspects of education and learning throughout the world, and this needs to be extended to corporations. This education enables business leaders to improve the mindsets of their employees, suppliers, vendors, and customers about the personal relevance of sustainability, the dangers of climate change and other social and environmental crises, and the urgent need for action. An informed population gives business and political leaders their mandate for change.

2. Lobby for replacing the GDP with a GPI.

A Genuine Progress Indicator (GPI)[vi] integrates health care, safety, environmental, and other indicators of well-being in conjunction with the Gross Domestic Product's (GDP's) financial and economic metrics to form a more holistic assessment of national progress. Endorsement of an annual report on national genuine wealth would legitimize value other than financial capital. Also, including an assessment of the national carbon or ecological footprint would awaken stakeholders to the need for urgent action on climate change and reinforce GPI as a strategy to boost corporate action and attention to these important issues.

3. Promote ecological tax shifting.

Much of our tax system is upside down; we are taxing positive actions and incentivizing negative actions. Instead of payroll taxes, which discourage new hiring, we should tax carbon to discourage pollution and waste. We should incent employment, renewables, capital investment, responsible consumption, and energy efficiency. Revenue-neutral shifting of taxes from things we do want to things we don't want will send strong behavioral-change signals to important corporate stakeholders.

4. Request elimination of "perverse subsidies."

Today, governments of industrial countries subsidize the fossil fuel industry with more than $200 billion annually. In 2005, between $29 and $46 billion of that went to the US fossil fuel industry alone.*vii* These are "perverse subsidies" because they subsidize environmentally destructive behavior. Citizens are billed twice for fossil fuels: once when their taxes pay for the subsidies and again when they bear the direct and indirect costs of environmental mitigation and health care costs. As with ecological tax shifting, perverse subsidies should be shifted from fossil fuel and nuclear industries to clean-tech industries.

5. Mobilize support for a price on carbon.

An effective carbon-price signal would exploit the power of market mechanisms to realize significant climate-change mitigation potential in all sectors. Most assessments suggest that carbon prices of $20 to $50/ton CO_2e, sustained or increased over decades, could lead to a power supply with significantly lower GHG emissions by 2050. This would also make many mitigation options more economically attractive, and would help further the financial potential of a cap-and-trade market.*viii* Governments should therefore cap carbon emissions by company, auction off permits, and let business either prosper or suffer. A carbon price is a crucial element of any plan to engage corporations in reducing greenhouse gases.

6. Lead by example.

We need corporate purchasing to increase the demand for "green" products from "green" suppliers. Businesses must lead by example by purchasing ENERGY STAR appliances, eco-friendly cleaning products, FSC certified paper with 100% post-consumer recycled fiber, recycled office products, advanced electric and hybrid vehicles with better fuel efficiency, and other similar "green" products and services. Corporations should also consider retrofitting or relocating to LEED certified buildings to save on energy costs, increase worker productivity, and improve employee health in the office. Most of all, we need businesses to show

how they are thriving by "greening" their supply chains, operations, products and services, to encourage others to join the bandwagon.

The business community can and will benefit by leading the climate revolution. Read on to see how. Then imagine how these bold actions would magnify those benefits.

Introduction

Like many of you, I had been hearing about climate change for years—and it was an issue that I cared about—but I didn't really see how I could make a difference on such a massive global issue. Although I cared about the increasingly scary rate at which glaciers are melting and the impact this is having on biodiversity and island nations, I struggled to relate to this issue because it didn't seem to impact my business or my day-to-day life.

My wife and I had already taken numerous actions to help, including buying a hybrid car, eating organic and local food, and buying environmentally friendly products. At work I was trying to make as much change as possible, but I felt like none of this was really going to make a significant difference in the grand scheme of things. So like many people, I tried to do my best and hoped that someone, anyone with power, would do something!

That all changed for me in January of 2007 after I read the first report from the Intergovernmental Panel on Climate Change (IPCC). I learned exactly how dire the situation was, and upon realizing that we had fewer than 10 years from that date to make decisive change, I found a new sense of urgency and purpose. I decided I was no longer going to sit back and wait for someone else to do something; I needed to get involved and in a big way.

It turns out that I wasn't the only one motivated by the IPCC's warnings. The report sparked a watershed moment for climate change, and soon after the report's release, the public and media for the first time really started to take climate change seriously, something that—as my wife points out—scientists had been screaming about for decades. Global warming began popping up on the cover of just about every major magazine and news program. Moreover, the business community shifted ever so slightly and began talking about this issue both at the water cooler and in corporate board rooms. That month, I decided to change the entire focus of my consulting business—its services, offerings, and policies—to focus on solving climate change.

Then as I traveled around the country in 2007 and 2008, working with clients and speaking to audiences, I realized that business leaders were looking for both a comprehensive understanding of how climate change might impact their companies and also a playbook for how to respond. The majority of the climate conversation up until that point had been focused on mega-topics like sea-level rise and the threat to polar bears, but very little had been done to tell companies how they could take action and improve their bottom-lines. Then when the financial crisis hit during the fall of 2008 the need became clear for a book that highlighted not only the numerous risks climate change poses for business but also the many opportunities for increased profitability; enhanced brand value; improved customer, employee, and shareholder relations; and better climate performance all at the same time – even during an uncertain and volatile economy.

That's where this book comes in.

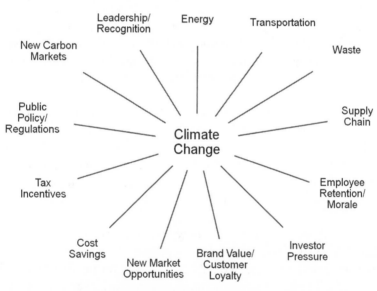

Figure 1. Climate change touches on every aspect of business operations and presents unique opportunities to make money and reduce costs.

For companies that approach climate change as an opportunity, there are many areas for strategic value creation. For companies that choose to ignore climate change, many of these same areas could become threats. Therefore I organized the book around these two divergent paths: I first highlight the business benefits of taking action on climate change by providing decision makers with both a "how to" and real world examples of companies that have profited by reducing carbon emissions. I then focus the second and third sections of the book on the various risks that companies face from potential carbon regulation and the market factors forcing business to take action, whether they want to or not.

That being said, I've written this book not because of a gloom-and-doom feeling that the world is coming to an end or that the economy is heading into a depression, but because I am filled with hope and enthusiasm, and have an eye on the enormous possibilities that climate change presents for companies and our society.

Business has always shown a propensity to mobilize its skills, talent, and resources to meet great challenges, especially when there is money to be made. While I wholeheartedly realize that American-style capitalism is largely responsible for getting us into this mess in the first place, I believe that as the markets, public policies, and consumer demand shift to make addressing climate change a priority, this same capitalist influence will be *the* key driver toward the change that is needed.

Climate change truly is the challenge of our generation. Generations from now, we will be measured and remembered for how we acted in the face of this massive problem. In a number of ways, I believe that this climate challenge can only be compared to the challenge faced by our parents and grandparents during World War II. We need the same type of commitment, but this time, instead of fighting fascism, we'll be heading off the greatest ecological and social disaster our planet has ever faced.

The generation that helped win WWII has been fondly referred to as "the greatest generation" because they stood tall against enormous odds and persevered. For our generation, the test is climate change.

We have both the responsibility and the opportunity to address this issue head-on. We need to be the ones to plant a flag in the ground and make a stand against global warming. For if we do, we will be the ones that our children and grandchildren will look back upon and thank for answering the call to duty. We can be *this* century's greatest generation.

As today's business leaders, we have the responsibility to respond, and this book will show you how to do so in a way that will reduce risk, increase profitability, meet customers' expectations, improve brand value, and save the planet all at the same time. This will be a great challenge, but it is solvable. We need bold action, and we need it today, not tomorrow. So join me in making this happen.

SECTION 1

ADDRESSING CLIMATE CHANGE: THE BUSINESS BENEFIT

There is both a necessity and numerous business opportunities exist for taking action on climate change. Throughout this section, I will cover what companies can do to reduce their carbon impact and provide both a process for implementation and real-world success stories of companies that have increased profitability, brand value, and their sustainability performance at the same time.

CHAPTER 1

THE CLIMATE IMPERATIVE

Humankind is faced with an unprecedented challenge. Never before has an ecological crisis presented as fundamental and serious a threat to our way of life on such a global scale as climate change. It seems that until recently, very few people—aside from climate scientists and a handful of environmentalists—paid attention to the greenhouse gases we were emitting into the atmosphere. I believe we are just now awakening to the reality of the situation.

We got into this situation because, over the past century, we have built our capitalistic market structure on two principles: an abundance of cheap fossil fuel energy and a focus on maximizing shareholder value in our business activity. These have been detrimental because, as market pressures have driven companies to focus on short-term profits, social and environmental impacts have only been considered insofar as necessary to avoid financial loss due to regulation.

I believe these principles are changing, and I believe climate change will be the driving force behind this change, because climate change is real, and people and corporations have begun to feel its impacts. Fossil fuels, especially oil, are no longer cheap, and the many costs of their extraction and use are on the rise. Additionally, consumer, market, and government pressures will no longer allow businesses to ignore their climate impacts. Before I get into the business case though, I first want to lay out the climate imperative and describe the environment in which your business will be operating.

Climate Change is Happening

The Intergovernmental Panel on Climate Change (IPCC), a consortium of more than 1,000 of the world's top scientists, stated that the "warming of the climate systems is unequivocal, as is now evident from observations of increases in global average air and ocean temperatures, widespread melting of snow and ice, and rising global average sea level."[ix] This statement leaves no room for doubt that the planet's temperature is increasing. Debate is now focused on how fast average temperatures will increase and what the full range of implications may be. Figure 2 is a graph that the IPCC created to show numerous models, using a range of estimates from conservative to aggressive:

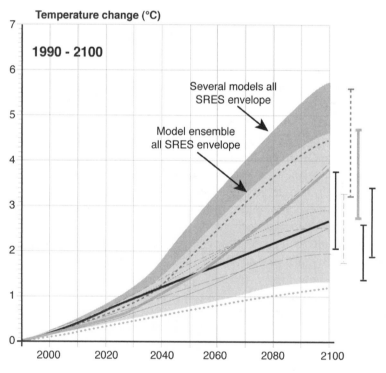

Figure 2. Models show that global temperatures are projected to increase.[x]

Though this model shows a considerable range in potential results from a minimum increase of 1.4 to a possible high of 5.8 degrees Celsius, it illustrates that, based on historical climate data, global temperatures will increase over the next century at the highest rate in the past 10,000 years. The extent to which this temperature increase occurs depends both on the changes that take place in natural systems and on human activity. Unfortunately, even the most aggressive numbers have proved to be understated. The first IPCC report predicted that the sea ice over the North Pole might be gone during the summer months of 2030, but now climatologists believe this may occur between 2008 and 2012.

Climate Change Impacts on Weather, Water, and Disease

Whether you believe in global warming or not is beside the point. Its effects are indisputable; all you have to do is look at the increased frequency and intensity of natural disasters. Although it may be that a portion of this trend comes from our increased awareness of disaster occurrences due to improvements in communication technology, the IPCC data suggests a very strong correlation between the recent changes in global temperatures and increases in extreme weather events.

Increase in Natural Disasters

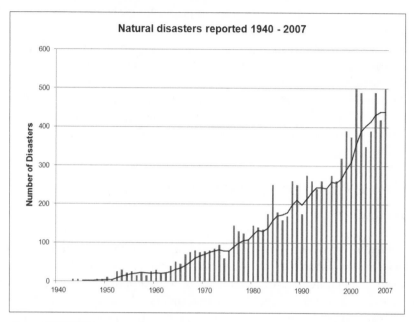

Source: ODFA/CRED International Disaster Database

Figure 3. Natural disasters reported globally since 1940 have increased.[xi]

Additionally, IPCC scientists agree that the health of millions of people is now at risk more than ever because of:

- More frequent and intense heat waves, floods, storms, fires, and droughts causing injury, disease, and death

- A decline in available potable water—and a simultaneous increase in world population

- An increase and spread of disease into previously uninfected geographies and countries[xii]

- The Centre for Research on the Epidemiology of Disasters (CRED) has identified several ways in which weather climate disasters have begun to worsen, including:

- Rainfall intensity;

- Storm intensity, especially hail, tornadoes and wildfire;

- Flood and drought;

- Effects of El Niño; and

- Loss of life and livelihood.[xiii]

Water Scarcity

Water scarcity has already begun to have considerable impact, especially in regions where people are already in crisis and conflict over this resource. Water scarcity is now becoming an issue for everyone throughout the world. Even in the United States, businesses have felt the pinch of increasing drought and diminishing water supply.

Water scarcity is being recognized as a risk to the entire global business community.[xiv] A nuclear power plant in Tennessee, for example, was forced to halt operations temporarily in 2007 because of a drought in the region. In California, the electronics industry alone consumes approximately 24 percent of the state's water. What will happen to the bottom lines of electronics companies as water becomes less available?

Several regions of the world, including the southwestern United States, have already reached "physical water scarcity," a condition in which more than 75% of river flows are allocated to agriculture, industry, or domestic purposes.[xv]

The global distribution of water is changing as well. According to estimates by the United Nations Environment Programme, one third of the world's population live in dry lands, which are threatened by desertification.[xvi] The livelihoods of more than 2 billion people are in jeopardy as farming and grazing land becomes increasingly parched. It doesn't take much imagination to realize that access to water will be increasingly important and, if not solved, may become a source of violent conflict.

Other Impacts

As a result of climate change and the increasing visibility of its effects, other related social and environmental concerns are increasing in both scope and severity. Ecosystems are in decline and resources are shrinking, and the potential impact to the planet's biodiversity is uncertain.

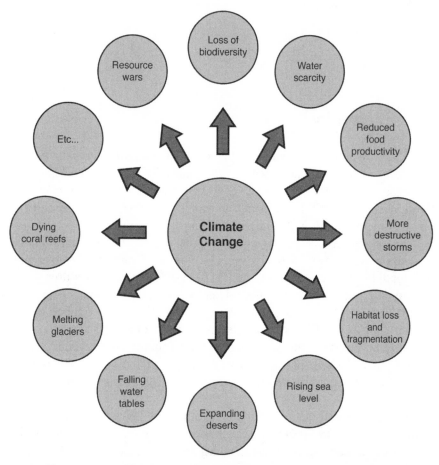

Figure 4. A sampling of the myriad of problems affected by climate change.

This is not sustainable. These impacts far exceed the world's true capacity to sustain life. NASA scientist James Hansen, one of the nation's premiere climatologists who testified in front of Congress more than 20 years ago about the threat of climate change, contends that we should be aiming to lower the concentrations of carbon dioxide in our atmosphere to 350 parts per million (ppm). Prior to the Industrial Revolution, carbon dioxide levels were at about 287 ppm, but as of 2008 we are at 387 ppm and are increasing at an estimated rate of 2-3 ppm per year.[xvii]

Conclusion

Although these statistics make for a dire picture, there is no need to feel hopeless. Climate leaders such as Al Gore and Bill McKibbon are confident that we can reduce to and stabilize at 350 ppm if business, government, and citizens get involved and take action.

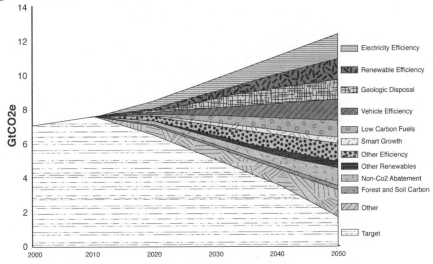

Figure 5. Wedges diagram adopted from Pacala and Socolow showing the necessary steps to reduce emissions.[xviii]

Thanks to the work of scientists and thought leaders like Hansen, Gore, McKibben, Pacala and Socolow among others, we are equipped with a roadmap to climate stabilization. We can clearly see what must be done, and business plays a tremendously important role. There is incredible profit to be made in the stabilization of our climate, and business leaders who see the situation for the exciting opportunities it holds will benefit from leading the charge. As you read farther into this book, you will see that there are many things you and your company can do to operate effectively in this new environment and be part of the solution to climate change, even in an uncertain economy.

CHAPTER 2

CARBON FOOTPRINTING

What is carbon footprinting, and how will it help my company? A carbon footprint—also referred to as an inventory—helps companies baseline their greenhouse gas emissions and gain an understanding of which aspects of their operations are carbon contributors. The carbon footprint is the first and most essential component of an emissions reduction strategy, providing a useful tool for managers to demonstrate inefficiencies in current operations. This chapter provides an overview of the carbon footprinting process, details what's involved, and offers examples for ways to communicate this process to employees.

The Carbon Footprint

A carbon footprint is a measurement of the amount of greenhouse gas emissions through the everyday operations of a business, creation of a product, or provision of a service. Each of the six major greenhouse gases (carbon dioxide, methane, nitrous oxide, sulfur hexafluoride, perfluorocarbons, and hydrofluorocarbons) has a different global warming potential, for example Methane is 21x more potent than CO_2. Therefore emissions are often converted to CO_2 equivalents (CO_2e) for ease of comparison. It is important to note that whenever you hear a company reporting its "carbon" or "CO_2" emissions what they are really referring to is CO_2 equivalents.

Although the methodology and scope will vary from footprint to footprint, in general, the emissions considered in the calculation should include direct emissions of energy, transportation, materials, freight, and waste. Calculating and tracking these organizational impacts can reveal areas where emission reductions can be made most efficiently and cost effectively and with the largest impact.

> "Performing a carbon footprint not only helped us get a handle on our emissions, but also pointed out a few other inefficiencies in our systems that we were able to correct and save a lot of money." —Kevin Hagen, REI[a]

The goal of this chapter is to give the reader a basic understanding and overview of the carbon footprint process and potential business benefit.

The Carbon Footprint Process

Steps to Conducting a Carbon Footprint

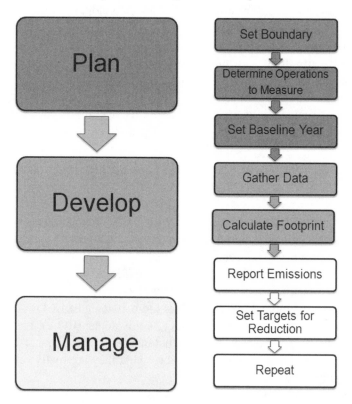

Figure 6. Sustainable Business Consulting's carbon footprint framework.

Plan

There are multiple ways to account for a company's total emissions. It all depends on what aspects of your company you want or need to include.

Setting Your Company's Organizational Boundary

Many larger organizations have subsidiaries, joint ventures, partnerships, franchises, or other business units that they may own a portion of but may or may not decide to include this affiliate's emissions as part of their carbon inventory. Therefore, before a company embarks on the data gathering exercise, it is important to know exactly what information needs to be gathered, and from what aspects of the business. This is up to each company to decide, but the World Resources Institute has defined three main ways to define the corporate footprint boundary.[xix]

BOUNDARY	EXPLANATION
Equity Share	Equity share means that the equivalent number of emissions from a subsidiary, joint venture, etc. in which a company has an equity stake are included in the inventory. If a company owns 100%, then all emissions are included, or if it only includes 51% ownership, then only 51% of the subsidiary's total emissions are included in the company's footprint.
Financial Control	A company has financial control "when [it] can direct its financial and operational policies to gain benefit from its activities."
Operational Control	A company has operational control "when [it] has the ability to implement and direct operating policies."

Potential carbon footprint scope boundaries, as defined by the World Resources Institute

There may be times when a company has financial control but not operational control, and vice versa. Once the company has decided on its boundary, it needs to be transparent and consistent going forward.

The company can also decide whether to include leased assets such as equipment or company vehicles. It may decide not to, or it may include these emissions even though it doesn't actually own the assets because the company is responsible for these emissions from day-to-day operations. Again, no matter which option you choose, it is important to set your boundary and stay consistent and transparent throughout the process.

As a company determines which emissions will and will not be included in your footprint, and why. You will need to think through each aspect of your business and decide where to draw the boundary—whether to include all of your operations; certain specific actions; the actions of your suppliers, customers, etc. If you are smaller or just getting started on your first footprint, many often start small with the actual areas that you control and not delve too deeply into the supply chain or customer issues for the baseline. However, I recommend including as much as possible in the first footprint to identify more opportunities for emission reduction and cost savings.

Determining Scopes:

Using the World Resources Institute (WRI) GHG Protocol, there are three distinct scopes of emissions:

- Scope 1: Direct Emissions. These are emissions your company directly owns, such as emissions from power generation on-site through boilers or furnaces for natural gas, or for fuel used in company-owned vehicles or fleets.

- Scope 2: Indirect Emissions. These are emissions from company operations and activities that are owned or controlled by another company such as electricity or steam from a utility.

- Scope 3: All other emissions, for example employee commuting.

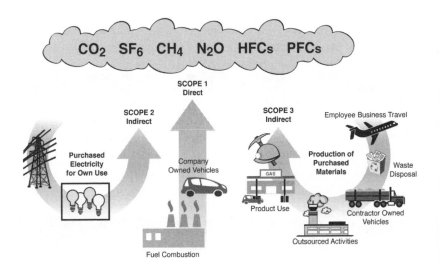

Source: World Resources Institute, adopted from NZBCSD, 2002

Figure 7. The World Resources Institute has defined three scopes for a carbon footprint.[xx]

Although I do not typically speak in terms of "scopes" because it can be confusing, I thought it important to use the terminology here because these are the established terminology from both the WRI and Climate Registry.

Most companies typically start with just their Scope 1 & 2 emissions and leave the more complicated footprinting for a later date. This is especially true for larger firms. Although, it won't be long before the public expects companies to include all aspects of operations, including the full supply chain.

Another way to decide which operational emissions to include is to break the emissions down to the five major business sources of emissions described in Figure 8. It is a little easier to communicate to the average person who is unfamiliar with the "scopes" terminology.

ENERGY: Electricity, natural gas, and steam	
Scope	GHG emissions associated with electricity and heating for your facilities.
Data Needs	Your energy bills and the type of energy you're using (e.g., electricity, natural gas, steam). Is your firm purchasing green power? Do your energy bills come through a central agency, or does each facility pay its own utility bills?

Who Has It	If you lease your facilities, you'll likely need to work with your landlord or building manager to get this data. If you own your facilities, accounting should have all the bills.
TRAVEL: Business travel, commuting, and company fleets	
Scope	GHG emissions associated with business travel and commuting.
Data Needs	Business travel information (e.g., miles traveled by airplane, car, bus, train, ferry). How much did your company spend on business travel last year in each of these categories?
Who Has It	Travel agency, accounting, travel department, office manager. If you need commuter data, you can collect this easily using an online survey tool.
WASTE: Solid (garbage), recycling, and compost	
Scope	GHG emissions associated with garbage, recycling, and compost.
Data Needs	Total quantities of trash, recycling, and composting.
Who Has It	If you lease your facilities, you'll need to get this data from the leasing company/ building manager. If you own your facilities, accounting should have all the bills from your waste hauler.
PAPER: Office paper for printers and copiers, bills generated for customers	
Scope	GHG emissions associated with paper consumption.
Data Needs	The quantity (number of reams or boxes) and type of copy and printer paper used (i.e., virgin, 30% or 100% recycled).
Who Has It	Procurement or office manager who orders/pays for office supplies. If you have a corporate account (e.g., with Staples or Office Depot), they should be able to put together a report for you.
FREIGHT: Movement of goods by ship, truck, train, and air	
Scope	GHG emissions associated with outbound shipping and inbound receiving.
Data Needs	Total pounds and miles traveled for each mode of transit, for both shipping and receiving.
Who Has It	Logistics manager, accounting.

Figure 8. The scopes of a basic carbon footprint, as developed by Sustainable Business Consulting.

Recreational Equipment, Inc (REI) Case Study:

The conventional wisdom for most US based outdoor retailers is that the largest contributor to its carbon footprint would be all the shipping and distribution of its product, notably from China. However, after performing its footprint, REI found out some surprising information in that its Adventure Travel business, which generates about the same revenue as one retail store, was responsible for 26% of the company's total carbon emissions. This is an excellent case study because it demonstrates the importance of measurement and what it can reveal, in REI's case that its largest source of emissions was something other than was expected.

Set the Baseline Year

After determining your organizational boundary and the scopes to measure, you need to determine the baseline year to track your emissions. This may be your most recent fiscal or calendar year, or it could be the year for which you have the oldest but most complete data, the turn of the century, or a significant business event such as a merger or acquisition. This is for each company to decide for themselves.

Gather Data

Data collection may be the most difficult part of the carbon footprint in part because most companies do not have existing or sufficient systems for tracking carbon-related information. Doing a carbon footprint requires tracking down all significant emissions released by the company, including energy, travel, waste, paper, and freight as listed above in Figure 8.

It helps you understand the type of information you need, some questions you will want to answer, and where to go within your firm to get information. Remember, the larger the company and scope, the longer this process will likely take.

Calculate Emissions

This step may sound easy, but because of the number of different tools out there and the varying methodologies that each use, it is important that your company choose a tool that follows accepted GHG methodology.

Although many free carbon calculators are available online, each one will give you different numbers using different emission factors. Additionally, some may only take into account Scope 1 and Scope 2 emissions, while others will vary greatly in what they include in their Scope 3 calculations. Also, it is often difficult to obtain the methodologies used by free online calculators. Some of the best tools and resources out there are the GHG Protocol of the WRI, the Climate Registry Information System (CRIS) of the Climate Registry, and the carbon inventory tool of the Seattle Climate Partnership.

Set a Target for Reduction

Once your carbon footprint has been calculated and analyzed, the next step is to set reduction goals and devise a strategy to achieve them. It is important to set clear goals, choosing specific reduction targets and a timeframe. These goals can be either absolute (e.g., 10% below 2008 levels) or intensity-based (e.g., 5% per employee).

The reduction target your company chooses may depend on your goals and the size and maturity of your business. Larger, more established companies that are focused on actual GHG reduction may choose an absolute reduction goal, whereas a fast-moving start-up growing at 200% annually may have to choose an intensity target in the short-term because it may struggle to reduce emissions below its historic emission numbers with that type of growth. This is up to the company.

Report Your Results

Once you have completed your footprint it is important to communicate the results of your footprint in terms that everyday employees and other stakeholders can understand. People who are less familiar with carbon footprinting might not have a clue as to what a pound of CO_2e represents or inherently understand how their actions can reduce emissions.

When my firm works with companies on carbon footprinting, we try to break certain emission indicators into per-employee numbers, to help break down the entire process into easier-to-understand metrics such as:

- CO_2 emissions/employee

- Kilowatt hours (kWh)/employee

- Therms/employee

- Paper usage/employee

- Business travel miles/employee

- Air travel miles/employee

- Average commuting miles/employee

- Pounds of waste/employee

I've also found that with every company I've worked with employees generally would like to lessen their environmental impact, but just don't see how their own individual actions will make much of a difference, especially inside larger companies. Employees want to understand how their individual actions can add up to something. This is especially true during volatile economic times, as managers need financial justification for their actions more than ever. In the table below, I have quantified a few easy individual actions that employees can take.

Sustainable Business Consulting

Carbon / Cash Saving Comparisons (on the next page)

If you Typically:	You Could:	Annual CO_2e Savings, Cost Savings		
Drive to work/ meetings alone (assume 10 mile commute)	Carpool	$1,521		
		Approx. 9 trees	2,293 lbs CO_2e	2,600 miles
	Take Public Transit	$1,560		
		Approx. 16 trees	4,099 lbs CO_2e	3,900 miles
	Bike or walk	$2,600		
		Approx. 18 trees	4,586 lbs CO_2e	5,200 miles

Carpool	Take Public Transit	$260/year		
		Approx. 7 trees	1,806 lbs/ CO_2e	1,300 miles
	Bike or walk	$1,300		
		Approx. 9 trees	2,293 lbs CO_2e	2,600 miles

Take public transit	Bike or walk	$1,040		
		Approx. 6 trees	1,433 lbs CO_2e	3,900 miles

Fly round trip to business meetings				
St. Louis to New York	Meet virtually	$381/trip		
		Approx. 8 trees	1,983 lbs CO_2e /trip	1,778 miles
San Francisco to New York	Meet virtually	$436/trip		
		Approx. 22 trees	5,510 lbs CO_2e /trip	5,160 miles

If you Typically:	You Could:	CO_2e Savings, Cost Savings	
Print and recycle paper	Commit to NO paper usage for the day	$31	
		Approx. 1 tree	193 lbs CO_2e

Leave computer on overnight	Turn off overnight	$20.8/CPU	
		Approx. 4 trees	921 lbs CO_2e

Drink bottled water	Switch to filtered tap water or water fountain	$364	
		Approx. 8.5 trees	2,106 lbs CO_2e

Buy coffee or other beverages	Use your own mug	65 lbs CO_2e	$26	Approx. 1/4 of tree

Use task lighting	Turn off at night	41 lbs CO_2e per bulb	$2.73	Approx. 1/4 of tree

Please note the fuel costs were calculated in 2008 using the Federal Mileage Reimbursement number of $0.50 per mile. The price of oil will likely cause this number to increase but we decided to use $0.50 to be conservative. Yearly averages are based on an estimated 260 work days/year. Actual savings will vary by office location, local pricing, distances traveled, etc. CO_2e = Carbon Dioxide Equivalents. All greenhouse gases have been converted to this common metric for ease of use: 1 car = 500 miles/800KM 1 tree = 250 lbs/112.5 Kg of CO_2e. Public Transit = Subway.

Obstacles to Watch for

Initially, the carbon footprint may seem overwhelming. Data collection and research may take time and resources, especially if a company has multiple accounting systems or if information is not tracked accurately. The good news is that all the work done for the first footprint to develop new tracking systems will make subsequent tracking and data gathering easier—especially if incorporated into existing reporting systems. Converting and analyzing the data may also be confusing at first, but once the systems are in place the process becomes standardized.

Another challenge is related to the various carbon footprinting guidelines. Fortunately, the standardization of GHG guidelines is occurring. Three major institutions that are experts in this field—the International Organization for Standardization (ISO) 14064 standards, the WRI, and the World Business Council for Sustainable Development (WBCSD)—are all collaborating to unite their work.[xxi] It is likely that as the cap-and-trade system comes to fruition in the US, these organizations will also join forces with the Climate Registry to produce a single national standard for the reporting of GHG emissions.

Conclusion

More and more companies are calculating their carbon footprints. As climate change awareness grows, this will be an increasingly important and regular part of doing business and will become as standard as annual financial statements. Carbon mitigation is a challenge that businesses are beginning to face and it will only grow in importance in the coming decades. Understanding where a company's emissions are coming from will help decision makers strategically reduce their environmental footprints as well as discover new efficiencies, new product and service opportunities, and potential cost savings even in an uncertain economy. In the next chapter you will see many of these benefits discussed in detail.

CHAPTER 3

BUSINESS BENEFIT

Many decision makers that I talk to ask me "how exactly will addressing climate change help my business?" This is an extremely valid question, especially given the state of the economy. I've found through my consulting work that the most effective way to answer this question is to provide real-world case studies of companies that have realized bottom-line business benefit from carbon reduction. This chapter provides a list of potential actions any company can take on climate change and highlights examples of companies across a range of industry sectors both private and public, from small to multinational, that have attained tangible financial, brand, and sustainability benefits by taking action on transportation, energy, waste, and materials.

Transportation

For many businesses, transportation is their most significant climate impact. This is especially true for retailers involved in the manufacturing and distribution of their products (i.e., complex supply chains) and service-based businesses that rely heavily on air travel.

> "Climate change will be a difficult challenge for all businesses. The good news is that there is incredible opportunity to be found and business can provide the innovation and profit motive to find tangible solutions that will make a difference." —Steve Leahy, CEO, Greater Seattle Chamber of Commerce[b]

For larger organizations, employee commuting is also a major source of emissions.

Despite the significant impacts resulting from transportation, the good news is that companies can do several things that are not disruptive to their operations to reduce GHG emissions.

For example, the innovations in virtual conferencing technology now provide an engaging and productive experience that can substitute all but the most important in-person visits requiring travel. And for that unavoidable travel, more and more car rental companies offer hybrids and other low-emission vehicles. Regarding employee commuting, we often hear "There is just no way I can get my employees out of their cars." In fact, a number of incentives have proven to do just that. Below are some examples of companies that have been successful in both regards.

Sun Microsystems [xxii,xxiii]

Sun launched its "Open Work" program, which gives employees the option to work at least part of the time from home. After 10 years, it has 20,000 participants—representing 56% of Sun's workforce—and has significantly enhanced productivity.

Financial	Brand	Sustainability
Realized cost-avoidance savings of more than $300 million Increased worker productivity by 34%	Developed a consulting practice to help other companies promote telecommuting	Has prevented nearly 29,000 tons of CO_2 emissions

Yakima [xxiv]

Yakima used to manufacture in Tijuana, Mexico, and then ship its products to its Memphis Distribution Center and then back to its customers on the west coast. This was costly both in time and fuel. Therefore, when it opened a west coast distribution center, it realized significant positive returns.

Financial	Brand	Sustainability
Saved $120,000 in fuel costs since inception	Cut transportation times by 50% getting its product to customers faster	Saved 40,000 gallons of fuel since inception

Ridolfi Inc.[xxv]

The small Seattle-based company recognized the significant climate impacts of air travel. Ridolfi worked to combine client trips and included carbon emissions in the criteria for determining whether or not to accept a job.

Financial	Brand	Sustainability
Saved $10,000 in air travel expenses	Demonstrated reduced costs to their clients through better travel policies	Reduced air mileage by 40%,significantly reducing company emissions

Additional Transportation-Related Actions Any Company Can Take

- Provide incentives to employees for not driving to work. Create a suite of things they could choose from, such as money toward gym memberships or cash for biking to work.

- Participate in a car-sharing program that can offer a wide range of vehicle types, including hybrids and fuel efficient compact cars and sedans.

- Offer free or reduced-cost transit passes.

- Maintain company vehicles. Replacing an old air filter can improve gas mileage as much as 10%; tuning up an engine can boost mileage as much as 4%; and keeping your tires properly inflated can provide an extra 3% more miles per gallon.

- Site new offices and developments near mass transit and in areas with both biking and walk-ability considered.

- Encourage the manager of your vehicle fleet to determine the most efficient transport routes and design a schedule according to these routes to be followed by all company drivers. UPS actually uses logistical software to minimize left turns, which reduces engine idling.

- Encourage the delivery of materials during non-peak traffic hours.

- Purchase or lease the most fuel-efficient vehicles when you swap out vehicles.

- Size your vehicle fleet according to your needs (i.e., use trucks for hauling, but drive around town in smaller, more fuel-efficient cars.

- Invest in videoconferencing and web-based meeting platforms to reduce air travel.

- Combine multiple client trips for all business travel.

- Enforce a "no idling" policy to ensure that company vehicles are turned off and not left to idle when they remain in one place for more than a few minutes.

Energy

Energy is also typically a large contributor to a company's carbon footprint. Since energy and fuel costs are volatile and remain largely out of the control of management, companies are striving to find any way possible to provide price stability and budget certainty. The best and most cost-effective way to do this is through energy efficiency, especially because major metropolitan cities and utilities are beginning to offer numerous incentives and reimbursements for businesses to become more energy efficient. Additionally, the EPA has a variety of energy-saving recommendations and incentives through its ENERGY STAR program.

Energy efficiency is also the cheapest new source of power and has the double benefit of reducing GHG emissions at the same time. All companies, large and small, can reap the benefits of an energy-efficiency strategy. Below are some examples of how:

DuPont[xxvi]

Employed numerous energy optimization technologies and techniques at its facilities, and worked to improve yields from its manufacturing processes. The company has seen positive results since the program started in 2004.

Financial	Brand	Sustainability
Over the course of its investments, it avoided costs of over $3 billion by keeping its energy use down, while expanding their businesses by 30%	Formerly notorious #1 polluter is now seen as an innovator	Reduced GHG emissions to 72 percent below 1990 levels Removed CO_2 emissions equivalent to almost 78,000 vehicles, or more than 900,000 barrels of oil

Lockheed Martin [xxvii,xxviii]

The company maximized use of day lighting and energy efficiency in the design of its Sunnyvale, California facility.

Financial	Brand	Sustainability
Saved $300,000 to $400,000 a year on energy bills	Employee productivity rose 15 % Won a $1.5 billion defense contract based on increased productivity	Used less fossil fuel-based electricity, reducing the company's carbon emissions

CP Property Management *(Now a Division of CBRE)*[xxix]

CP installed smart-time optimization programming and turned off HVAC systems on Saturdays for three of its Seattle Properties.

Financial	Brand	Sustainability
Saved $51,265 in 2007 on electricity bills alone	Used this as part of its "green" property management branding strategy	Saved over 3,939,372 kWh in electricity in 2007

River Run Bed and Breakfast Kerrville, TX[xxx]

Installed a high-efficiency heat pump and individual zone controls for heating and cooling in occupied areas and added programmable thermostats and ceiling fans in guest rooms.

Financial	Brand	Sustainability
Saved $2,400 a year with a six-month payback	Guests expressed increased satisfaction in the quality and comfort of the inn	Prevented 77,451 pounds of CO_2 emissions annually

Columbus Hospitality Group Columbus, OH[xxxi]

Upgraded lights to CFLs, installed high-efficiency air conditioning units in guest rooms, replaced most water circulation pumps with high-efficiency pumps. They also added occupancy sensors and installed water-saving showerheads, toilets, and sinks.

Financial	Brand	Sustainability
Saved an estimated $30,000	Realized increased patient satisfaction	Saved 480,000 kWh since the start of the program

Additional Energy-Related Actions Any Company Can Take

- Protect windows from sunrays with large overhangs and double-pane glass.

- Control heat, air, and moisture leakage by sealing windows and doors.

- Turn down the thermostat by as little as one degree in cold weather to save as much as 1–2% on the energy bill.

- Clean or replace dirty air conditioner filters as recommended.

- Set a timer for air conditioning and heating units. Time them to come on a short time before people come into the office and to turn off shortly after everyone leaves.

- Turn off air conditioning and heating when the building is not being used (i.e., Saturday and Sunday and holidays).

- Install compact florescent light (CFL) bulbs. They require ¼ of the energy for the same level of luminescence and last 10 times as long.

- Make sure that any new office hardware that is purchased is either refurbished or meets ENERGY STAR's new E-80 standard.

- Install motion detectors in individual offices and in conference rooms to ensure that the lights are on only when people are present. Utilities often provide rebates for each motion detector purchased.

- Invest in flat-screen LCD monitors. They not only draw less energy but also release less heat than boxy monitors, which decreases your need for air conditioning.

- Dust the lights to increase brightness.

- Conduct an energy audit of lighting and HVAC systems.

- Monitor, record, and post rates of energy and water use. Watch for changes that may indicate a need to repair or change equipment.

- Encourage staff to close drapes and turn off lights and air conditioning when rooms are unoccupied.

- Replace all exit signs with light-emitting diode (LED) exit signs. These high-efficiency exit signs can save $15–$20 in electricity costs when compared with typical, incandescent signs.

- Disconnect unused ballasts where fluorescent tubes have been removed, as they still draw significant amounts of energy even though the tubes have been removed.

- Ensure that all staff are trained in good practice (e.g., waste segregation, lighting and heating control) and that relevant issues are included in induction training. Carry out refresher training once a year.

- Use day lighting where possible. Consider skylights in the ceiling and glazing with light shelves around the perimeter.

- Use ceiling fans to reduce the use of air conditioners.

- Install software that will allow downloads in the evening from the IT department but then put the computers back into the sleep mode for the rest of the night.

- Set PCs to power down when not in use.

- Research power providers in the area and select a provider that guarantees that a fraction of its delivered electric power is derived from net nonpolluting renewable technologies.

Materials

Every company is unique in the materials its uses. Whether a company is in the retail, service, or manufacturing sector, it can consider ways to reduce material usage, recycle, or substitute more environmentally friendly materials. The solutions are as diverse as:

1. Finding ways to use less "stuff"—in manufacturing, delivery, and packaging.

2. Using recycled or reusable materials.

3. Identifying biodegradable substitutes.

The steps each company takes will vary widely across industries, but the examples below highlight potential actions and the ways they save businesses money, improve the brand image, and lower GHG emissions all at the same time.

Wendel Rosen Black & Dean [xxxii]

This company switched from 30% to 100% post-consumer, chlorine-free recycled paper in its products.

Financial	Brand	Sustainability
The move actually cost a little more money up front	Become the first law firm in the country to gain third-party certification as a "Green Business"[xxxiii]	Eliminated 40,000 pounds of CO_2, Saved 250 trees, 24,000 gallons of water, and 33,000 kWh of electricity - enough power to run 3.4 homes for a year[xxxiv]

General Mills Hamburger Helper [xxxv]

This division changed production from curly noodles to straight noodles and then redesigned packaging to shave 20% off the size of its packaging.

Financial	Brand	Sustainability
Reduced the cost of raw materials packaging by 10%[xxxvi]	Demonstrated to customers a simple, easy solution to reduce GHG emissions without any impact on consumer behavior	Fuel savings equated to 500 fewer distribution trucks on the road each year

Unilever [xxxvii]

It reconfigured the plastic bottles for its Suave shampoo.

Financial	Brand	Sustainability
Saved more than $2 million in diesel costs alone	Met the stricter packaging requirements of customers such as Wal-Mart	Shampoo: Saved plastic equivalent to some 15 million bottles a year

Verizon Communications Inc., NY [xxxviii]

Switched to a paperless billing service promoting online forms, training and electronic purchase orders.

Financial	Brand	Sustainability
Saved $5.4 million in paper processing and printing costs and reduced administrative costs by $3.7 million	More than 3 million customers participated in Verizon's online paperless billing service since inception	Decreased office paper use by 1,300 tons from the use of online forms, and electronic purchase orders saved an additional 47.5 tons of paper

Additional Materials-Related Actions Any Company Can Take

- Use duplex printing and copying whenever possible or, for in-house documents, print on the clean side of used paper. Paper currently represents more than 70% of office waste.

- Buy recycled paper. Production of post-consumer recycled paper can use 2/5 of the energy of the virgin alternative.

- Ensure that all kitchen cleansers, paper towels, and napkins are 100% biodegradable. Work with the landlord to get the cleaners to use 100% biodegradable chemicals such as those available from Coastwide Laboratories of Corporate Express.

- Where possible, try to purchase local products and materials. This cuts down on the environmental damage of packaging, storage, and transportation and helps support local business, enhancing community relationships and goodwill.

- Take an active role in influencing and working with suppliers. Utilize stricter environmental, climate, social, and fair-labor policies in your vendor contracts and request for proposals (RFPs) to encourage suppliers to use more sustainable products.

- Provide reusable crockery and cutlery instead of disposables in the office kitchen.

- Purchase from local suppliers and vendors whenever possible.

- Encourage the use of e-mail for both internal and external communication or, if this is not possible, circulate material rather than making copies for individuals.

- Ask your contractors to use materials having low volatile organic compounds (VOCs) content during renovation.

- Communicate to your suppliers and vendors what you are doing. Get them to measure their carbon footprints and require them to complete applicable footprint data in their timesheets and reimbursement forms.

Waste

Anything that doesn't provide value to your customer is waste. Therefore, any reduction in waste that a company can uncover represents a profit-improvement opportunity. Sustainable-design pioneers Michael Braungart and Bill McDonough base their philosophy on the idea that "waste equals food."

Although we fully believe this to be true, we have found that the average business owner or manager doesn't often think in these terms. I therefore use the phrase "waste equals money," because when you dispose of something, you are throwing away money. In fact, opportunities to capture waste streams and turn them into new revenue streams are being promoted through an emerging practice known as industrial ecology. This is discussed in more detail in Chapter 10 but in industrial ecology, businesses partners use the waste from one company as the raw materials for another. This is an efficient way to get the most out of our resources and divert waste and pollution from our landfills and environment. An example of this was when Ben & Jerry's decided to sell its dairy waste to local pig farmers. It removed this costly waste from its bottom line and turned it into a valuable resource for the farmers, thus turning a cost center into a profit center on the income statement.

Because the majority of waste in the US ends up in landfills—which are large contributors to methane emissions (which I mentioned in Chapter 2 are twenty-one times more potent than CO_2) - any waste that is eliminated positively impacts a company's carbon footprint as well as its bottom line.

All kinds of companies have successfully reduced waste and realized positive returns on carbon performance. Many of these measures are cheap and easy to implement, making waste a good place for many companies to start addressing climate change.

Garvey Schubert Barer ^{xxxix}

The firm's Seattle office made a dramatic shift away from paper. It installed six high-speed scanners to scan every paper correspondence coming into the office and switched from paper storage to a web-based system. This reduced off-site storage and rental costs and opened up six rooms per floor for use or sublease.

Financial	Brand	Sustainability
Total net savings since inception = more than $1,000,000 from reclaimed office space, paper costs, and employee time (including filing, copying, shredding, storage, and retrieval)	Helped the firm become recognized as one of the most sustainable law firms in Seattle	Dramatically reduced the amount of paper used, stored, and disposed of

Idaho National Laboratory

The lab replaced disposable paper cleaning wipes with reusable cloth towels, bought retreaded tires for vehicles, and started recycling tires that could not be retreaded.

Financial	Brand	Sustainability
Saved $21,000 annually by eliminating paper waste	Maintained its image as a leader in engineering and the environment	Diverted hundreds of tons of waste from landfills
Saved $60,000 annually on tires		

Cascade Designs ^{xl}

Turned the waste foam from its Therm-a-Rest camping mattresses into the raw materials for a new line of camp pillows.

Financial	Brand	Sustainability
Turned a disposal cost into a revenue stream.	Developed a value-added product to meet customer demand	Repurposed tons of waste foam destined for the landfill annually

Burgerville, OR[xli]

Implemented a food composting and recycling program in all 39 of its restaurants.

Financial	Brand	Sustainability
Saved $100,000 annually in hauling fees across its system	The employee-led program allowed employees to feel empowered and contribute their creativity and passion in their daily work	Initial waste analysis found the restaurant could divert 85 percent of their waste out of landfills

Additional Waste-Related Actions Any Company Can Take

- Pay bills online and utilize direct deposit to save on paper use as well as mailing costs and envelopes.

- Separate waste at the source, rather than going through all the trash after it is collected. For example, provide containers for recyclables in office areas and compost bins in kitchen areas.

- Work with other businesses and organizations and the local municipality to support the development of efficient waste separation, collection, recycling, and compost systems.

- Install water-saving faucets, shower heads, and faucets and devices such as low-flush toilets. Low-flow fixtures can reduce the flow of water by 50 percent without affecting the comfort level of the user.

- Don't ignore leaks. A leaky faucet or dish washer, or a stuck solenoid valve that loses one-tenth of a gallon per minute will waste more than 50,000 gallons of water a year.

- Recycle paper, plastic, aluminum, and ink cartridges. Companies such as Staples offer $3 store credit for individual printer cartridges.

- Reuse packing materials and cardboard boxes.

- Switch to rechargeable batteries. Large office supply stores even have collection centers for recycling dead rechargeable batteries.

- Donate or recycle old computers and equipment.

- Keep up with regular maintenance of all mechanical equipment.

- Stop junk mail by registering with the site Lose 41 lbs (www.41pounds.org/).

- Include waste-minimization and waste-management procedures in staff induction training and ongoing staff training.

- Utilize native plants in landscaping to reduce water usage

> "Climate change will be the defining issue of this generation. You cannot underestimate the potential inspirational & productivity benefits of having an engaged workforce believing that the work that they are doing is helping address this global catastrophe." Mark Albion [c]

Integration into Existing Company Practices

For a company to reap the full financial benefits of a climate change strategy, including all the derivative and co-benefits, the strategy must be carefully and fully integrated. It is important to make a serious commitment and incorporate the following three strategies into your carbon reduction strategy to maximize the business benefit.

- Leadership from senior management

-Include climate change in the corporate mission, vision , and goals
-Reinforce it as a business strategy vs. compliance or PR
-Communicate support clearly in speeches, memos, actions, etc.

- Educate the whole company

-Train all employees in climate change and sustainability
-Involve employees by soliciting ideas or creating friendly competitions between departments

- Align with management systems

-Integrate into reviews, recognition, and reward systems
-Align with current measurement systems

Conclusion

Profitability and climate performance are not at odds with one another, and companies have numerous options to improve their climate performance while saving money and improving their brand value at the same time.

Beginning with the easy, low hanging fruit is the first step, but the more comprehensively a company integrates a carbon reduction strategy into its overall corporate practices the greater the potential business benefit it will reap.

CHAPTER 4

RETURN ON SUSTAINABILITY (ROS)

Business leaders need to prioritize climate change efforts and understand what return they are going to get from these investments. This chapter is designed to provide decision makers with both a framework for how to sort through the implementation process and real world examples of companies that have realized financial and brand benefit by reducing carbon emissions.

To help companies sort through the myriad of potential strategies and opportunities for reduction, and to quickly help them understand which actions give them the most 'bang for the buck,' I've created a new framework called Return on Sustainability (ROS) and several new carbon ratios to give decision makers quantifiable tools to quickly assess and compare their sustainability performance.

> "In addition to the financial returns on climate change, there will be additional benefits around CSR reporting, insurance, debt and equity markets, supply chain and brand value." —Gifford Pinchot, President, Bainbridge Graduate Institute[d]

These quantifiable metrics are important because, as we and others have tried to do this work, we have run into the following responses from our employees, managers, executives, and boards:

- "I have to worry about the bottom line first."

- "We can't afford to do this right now!"

- "It will cost more."

- "I don't deal with environmental issues."

- "I'm expected to produce each quarter, and with everything going on, climate really isn't a priority."

- "Even if we do the best we can, there'll still be backlash from environmentalists, so why bother?"

In response to these concerns, my firm, Sustainable Business Consulting (SBC), developed the ROS framework. The ROS calculates the financial, brand, and carbon impacts of each potential action a company may take in response to climate change and gives decision makers the prioritized, actionable, and quantified information they need to do their jobs.

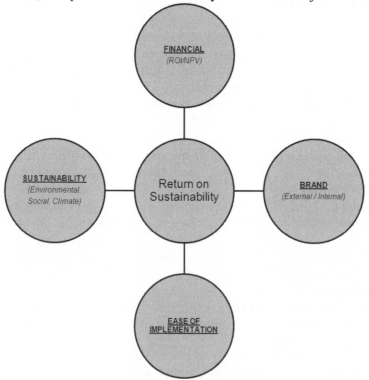

Figure 9. The Return on Sustainability framework helps businesses understand the full spectrum of benefits associated with their carbon-reduction strategy.

The ROS process is based upon some of the work of John Elkington's Triple Bottom Line (TBL) theory, which measures social, economic, and environmental parameters.*xlii* However, as I've consulted with companies about climate change, I've found that businesses want help taking action on climate but are more focused on actions that contribute to their bottom line , that add brand value, are easy, and are not nearly as interested in the social aspect of the TBL.

Language and Buy-in

Companies are under pressure to juggle a staggering number of business priorities, and in this economic environment you would not expect to see climate change at the top of the list in very few of them. As Figure 10 shows and the rest of the book will describe in detail, however, climate change and a company's reaction to it will affect each and every one of these business priorities.

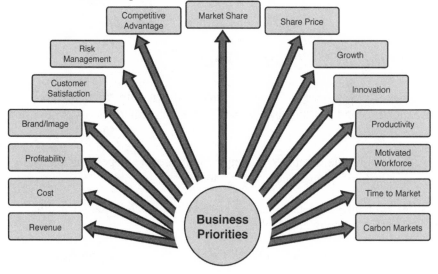

Figure 10. Climate change affects each of these business priorities.

One of the key lessons the ROS is built on is that managers need to be able to communicate climate change and sustainability-related information in the language of business. One of the primary reasons so many social, environmental, and climate initiatives experience resistance inside businesses is that the issues are not being discussed in terms that are important to managers today. For example, when discussing climate change with a marketing manager, one should be able to show how a climate message will resonate with target consumers and will provide the company with competitive advantage and market differentiation. When discussing it with a CFO, you need to be able to demonstrate the financial benefits because profitability is essential to all businesses, and without positive cash flow, companies cannot implement many of their climate and sustainability goals.

That's why my firm developed and employs the ROS process. I believe it is the most effective measure for determining and understanding the best actions for a company to take toward GHG emission reduction; it provides a quantitative score across categories and is weighted based on a company's own goals and objectives. From those calculations, the ROS delivers a strategic road map, with prioritized implementation for actions that will improve the company's financial, brand, and sustainability performance.

How the ROS Process Works

The ROS process, which is broken down into four categories—Financial, Brand, Sustainability, and Ease of Implementation—is designed to

- Allow the company to weigh each category depending on its level of importance to the company,

- Quantify and put real numbers behind each potential action the company could take,

- Score each action across all four aspects and by category, and

- Discover low-hanging fruit for immediate action to increase buy-in throughout the firm.

The exact items that are included in the calculations are scored based on their impact in each category and are detailed below.

Financial

- Up-front costs
- Net Present Value and Return on Investment
- Payback period

Brand

External

- Ability to increase existing customer satisfaction and loyalty
- Ability to generate new customers in the market place
- Importance to stakeholders such as suppliers, vendors, and shareholders
- Ability to capture market share from competitors

Internal

- Impact on workplace productivity and employee morale
- Effect on employee retention and recruitment

Sustainability

- Emissions reduction potential
- Environmental benefit
- Social and community benefits

Ease of Implementation

- Identify low-hanging fruit and possible immediate actions

- Determine areas of difficulty and resistance such as company culture, financial constraints, time, and resources

ROS Process

To conduct an ROS at your company, you'll want to put together a cross-functional team because you'll not only be able to come up with more potential actions but also have a deeper knowledge base to draw on to score each action. When I work with companies, I try to get representatives from as many of these departments as possible: management, accounting, IT, marketing and PR, facilities, operations, manufacturing, product design, customer service, legal, community relations, philanthropy, purchasing, supply-chain, and environmental affairs. Not every company will have each of these roles, and you may not be able to get all of these people in the same room at the same time, but the more interdisciplinary the team, the better.

Step 1: Brainstorm all potential carbon-reduction actions the business could take, from the smallest and easiest to the largest and boldest
The areas for action shown in column one of the scorecard below are guides to help get you thinking about all the areas within your company where action could be taken. This should cover the full range of company activities, departments, business units, and products. Some companies may choose to list each of their departments in this column and design actions specific to their corporate structure, and if you aren't sure, Chapter 3 provides lists for many areas that may help get you going in creating your own set of possible actions.

Step 2: Set the Weights
The company decision makers need to weight each of the four impact categories based on the areas of most importance to them. In the example scorecard below, which is for a law firm, management places more emphasis on the financial performance and brand value than on the sustainability and ease of implementation components. I find that most

companies tend to weight the ease and financial categories the highest: Business leaders want to know "What can we get done today?" and "What's going to give us the best bang for our buck?"

Step 3: Score Each Action

This is where you will rely on the expertise in the room, as people will have to work together to figure out the impact each potential action may have. Each action needs to be given a score of 1–10 in each impact category, with 1 being the lowest benefit and 10 being the highest benefit. These scores then need to be combined for each activity based on the weights.

Step 4: Analyze in Depth

Now that you've done the back-of-the-envelope scoring, it's time to truly analyze the financial, brand, and emissions-reduction impacts that each action may bring. This is done outside of the group setting so each person from the team can go back and run the numbers for each score and talk to their stakeholders to verify and adjust as needed.

Step 5: Re-score and Sort

Now that you've analyzed the numbers in depth and re-scored the items, you will want to compare the scores. Obviously, the actions with the best combined scores are the ones that will have the biggest total benefit to your firm and are the ones to put at the top of your priority list.

Step 6: Sort by Category

There will always be some bias toward implementation in a particular impact category, and one of the benefits of the ROS process is that it enables you to also look at the scores in each impact category, so that if your firm wants to know what actions have the highest scores within just one particular impact category, you can find out that information as well.

Step 7: Strategize and Implement

Now that you've completed the scorecard and have vetted and quantified each action by its financial return, carbon reduction opportunity, brand benefit, and ease of implementation, you can set about developing a strategy for implementation.

Example ROS Scorecard

This example score card is based on a law firm. For simplicity we list two action items per business area but expect that you would come up with many more actions when you brainstorm for your company.

POTENTIAL ACTIONS	IMPACT CATEGORIES				
	FINANCIAL	BRAND	SUSTAINABILITY	EASE	SCORE
Weight assigned:	60%	25%	10%	5%	100%
Operations					
Print/copy all documents double sided	5	4	8	9	5.25
Replace light bulbs with CFLs	7	2	8	8	5.90
Shareholders					
Annual reports sent out electronically	7	5	8	7	6.60
Pursue SRI investors	2	7	8	4	3.95
Supply Chain / Vendors					
Questionnaire sent to supply chain about its climate efforts	1	7	6	8	3.35
Educate all vendors about company climate efforts	2	3	3	6	2.55
Employees / HR					
Employees given free bus passes	3	3	7	7	3.60
Offer $25 week for bikers to work	5	3	8	6	4.85
Products / Services					
Reduce toxic chemicals in products by 25%	3	8	7	2	4.60
Create one carbon neutral product by 2009	2	7	9	2	3.95
Marketing/Advertising					
Move 50% of all advertising to electronic/web	4	9	6	3	5.40

Match philanthropy w/marketing strategy	8	6	9	6	7.50
Environmental Affairs					
Obtain ISO 14000 certification	2	3	8	2	2.85
Perform carbon footprint for entire company	2	3	7	5	2.90
Community / Social					
Staff offered 25 hours of community volunteer time	4	7	8	5	5.20
Obtain Accountability 1000 standard	2	7	7	3	3.80
Management					
Management retreat done virtually instead of travel	8	2	8	4	6.30
Risk Reduction					
Prepare for future CO_2 regulation (legal, regulatory, labor)	4	4	6	7	4.35
Double number of safety trainings	3	2	7	8	3.40

Of course, for each company, the weight or the importance they want to assign to each of the categories will differ. That is one of the strengths of the ROS — it can be completely tailored to each individual company's values and goals.

Let's try the same example, but change the weighting system so that Financial is worth 50%; Sustainability, 40%; Brand, 5%; and Ease of Implementation, 5%. As you can see below, the scores come out differently.

BUSINESS AREA	FINANCIAL	BRAND	SUSTAINABILITY	EASE	SCORE	
Weight assigned:	50%	5%	40%	5%	100%	+/-
Operations						
Print/copy all documents double sided	5	4	8	9	6.9	**1.65**
Replace light bulbs with CFLs	7	2	8	8	7.1	**1.2**
Shareholders						
Annual reports sent out electronically	7	5	8	7	7.2	**0.6**
Pursue SRI investors	2	7	8	4	5.3	**1.35**
Supply Chain / Vendors						
Questionnaire sent to supply chain about its climate efforts	1	7	6	8	5.0	**1.65**
Educate all vendors about company climate efforts	2	3	3	6	3.3	**0.75**
Employees / HR						
Employees given free bus passes	3	3	7	7	5.4	**1.8**
Offer $25 week for bikers to work	5	3	8	6	6.2	**1.35**
Products / Services						
Reduce toxic chemicals in products by 25%	3	8	7	2	4.9	**0.3**
Create one carbon neutral product by 2009	2	7	9	2	5.3	**1.35**
Marketing/Advertising						
Move 50% of all advertising to electronic/web	4	9	6	3	5.1	**-0.3**
Match philanthropy w/marketing strategy	8	6	9	6	7.8	**0.3**
Environmental Affairs						
Obtain ISO 14000 certification	2	3	8	2	4.5	**1.65**

Perform carbon footprint for entire company	2	3	7	5	4.7	**1.8**
Community / Social						
Staff offered 25 hours of community volunteer time	4	7	8	5	6.1	**0.9**
Obtain Accountability 1000 standard	2	7	7	3	4.7	**0.9**
Management						
Management retreat done virtually instead of travel	8	2	8	4	6.6	**0.3**
Risk Reduction						
Prepare for future CO_2 regulation (legal, regulatory, labor)	4	4	6	7	5.4	**1.05**
Double number of safety trainings	3	2	7	8	5.5	**2.1**

Employing the ROS strategy is an effective framework for companies wondering how best to lower their emissions and how to get the best return from financial and brand perspectives at the same time. It removes some of the guesswork and places less emphasis on conventional wisdom or anecdotal thinking, providing decision makers with an in-depth quantified analysis that includes all the major functions of the organization.

The Importance of Activity-Based Costing

As we mentioned earlier, managers sometimes have difficulty justifying action on climate change because the up-front cost for the more environmentally friendly product or service may be slightly higher. Thus, it is important to explore which costs are being included and which are not, because too often, only the initial costs are considered, and not the operating or total life-cycle costs. For this reason, it is important to use Activity-Based Costing (ABC), which is the process of assigning overhead costs based on the resources required for each product or service in a company's operations.

I am adamant about using ABC in the ROS process because carbon-reduction actions make smart business sense. Take, for example, a CFL bulb: It costs more up front and would never be chosen if initial cost was the only criteria considered. The fact that this light bulb lasts about 10 times as long and saves about $30 in energy over its lifetime makes it a cost saver in the long term.*[xliii]* Once you include the indirect costs of storage, and maintenance for swapping out the older incandescent bulbs, the true cost savings makes the switch to CFLs a no-brainer.

Another good example of ABC's importance is waste disposal. If waste is tracked only in terms of the direct costs, it may only show up on one line item on financial statements. However, there are many indirect costs, including labor for collection, transportation, processing and sorting, and storage. If a product contains any toxic or hazardous substances, there may be additional costs including:

- Permit fees

- Monitoring

- OSHA/safety costs

- Liability insurance

- Workers' compensation premiums

- Potential health impact

If all of these expenses are included in a cost-benefit analysis, the preferred course of action may look quite different than if only the direct cost of waste disposal is considered.

Another example where by using ABC you may make a better informed decision involves Coastwide Laboratories of Washington, now part of Corporate Express. It produces environmentally safe and biodegradable cleaning products. The company has been able to demonstrate a cost savings with their product even though the price per gallon is usually higher than competitors' traditional products. The reason customers save money by using their products is that less product is needed per application because it evaporates more slowly: Even though per-gallon costs are higher, less product is needed. Also, because Coastwide cleaners are environmentally safe, no special storage or handling is required by workers, which means no money is spent on latex gloves and masks and workers' compensation premiums are lower for the cleaning company because workers are not handling harmful chemicals.

Activity-based costing gives a more accurate picture based on the total costs of a particular product or service rather than considering only up-front and direct costs, and enables better financial decision making.

New Carbon Metrics

Financial indicators are the predominant mechanism for assessing companies' profitability, efficiency, and financial health; they help investors, analysts, and internal financial officers quickly determine company performance. The same needs to be true for carbon accounting because these same people will need quick and easy ratios to understand, evaluate, and communicate their companies' climate performances. To address this need, and to support the work we've detailed above with both the ROS and activity-based costing, my firm has developed the new set of carbon metrics shown in Figure 11.

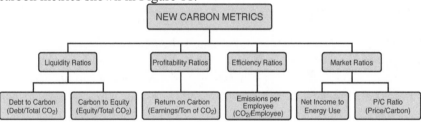

Figure 11. Carbon metrics to help companies manage carbon as it relates to their bottom lines.

CARBON METRICS USE	WHO IS HELPED
• Assess the climate performance of companies over time • Compare the climate performance of different companies against each other • Quickly assess performance without having to do a full carbon footprint	• Current and potential investors • Business analysts Internal managers

Carbon metrics enable decision makers to quickly compare a company's climate performance and help uncover areas of concern. These ratios serve as benchmarks to help track a company's carbon progress over time and evaluate how efficiently the company uses carbon emissions to generate revenue and increase shareholder value. Additionally, business analysts and current and potential investors can use the ratios to evaluate the climate-change performance of a particular business or sector, especially in comparison to competitors.

I believe that as the economy becomes increasingly carbon constrained and as regulations, taxes, and external parties such as insurance companies, suppliers, and financial institutions inquire about carbon performance, these ratios will become even more important indicators of a company's climate performance. This is especially true as carbon footprinting, corporate social responsibility (CSR), and Socially Responsible Investing (SRI) become more sophisticated and common.

Below are descriptions of each metric and how they can be calculated.

Return on Carbon

The Return on Carbon ratio measures the amount of greenhouse gases a company emits to generate earnings. A high rate would indicate that a company is very efficient at generating profits per unit of carbon dioxide; a lower rate equates to inefficiency and a higher carbon output than necessary.

$$\frac{\text{Net Income}}{CO_2} \text{ ex:} \quad \frac{3,000,000}{40,000} \quad = 75$$

Debt-to-Carbon

The debt-to-carbon ratio enables decision makers to understand how much debt is being financed to produce the company's carbon emissions. A low debt-to-carbon ratio indicates that the company is efficient at using debt to finance its carbon-emitting operations. A higher number indicates less efficiency. For example: A number below 10 indicates efficiency, but a number above 30 indicates inefficiency.

Debt _____   ex: $\underline{400,000}$ = 10:1
Total CO_2 40,000

Carbon-to-Equity (C/E)

The carbon-to-equity ratio can be used to determine the relative proportion of greenhouse gas emissions to equity. A smaller number indicates to shareholders that the company is emitting a low amount of emissions to generate equity. A higher number indicates that a company has to generate a higher rate of emissions to generate equity value.

Total CO_2 ___   ex: $\underline{40,000}$ = 0.1
Equity   400,000

Emissions per Employee

This calculation measures the greenhouse gas emissions per employee, enabling a comparison of climate impact among businesses of different sizes. It is also helpful to a growing company that wants to know how its carbon performance compares to its increase in employee head count. A lower number indicates fewer emissions per employee, which might be good for fast-growing companies that may struggle to reduce their overall carbon emission but want to reduce their emission per employee.

Metric Tons CO_2e ___   ex: $\underline{4,000}$ = 4 $MTCO_2e$/employee
Employee   1,000

Carbon-to-Price (C/P)

The carbon-to-price ratio is a measure of the price paid for a share of the firm relative to the greenhouse gas emissions per share. This is similar to a price-to-earnings ratio. A higher C/P ratio indicates that investors are paying more for each unit of carbon, so a lower number is preferred.

Metric Tons of Carbon ___   ex: $\underline{4,000}$ = 80
Price per Share $50

Net Income to Energy Consumed

This is the ratio of profit to energy consumption. It directly links income to energy use and tracks how much money is being made per unit of energy consumed. As energy prices increase, finding ways to be more energy efficient will increase in importance. In this ratio, the higher the number, the more efficient the company is with its energy use, while the lower the number, the more the company should be encouraged to look at its energy-use practices.

$$\frac{\text{kWh}}{\text{Net Income}} \quad \text{ex:} \quad \frac{100{,}000}{3{,}000{,}000} \quad = \quad \$0.03 \text{ per kWh}$$

Limitations

These metrics should not be used as a substitute for rigorous financial and carbon analysis, because, similar to financial indicators, these carbon metrics are only as valuable as the transparency with which the data is reported. As I mentioned in Chapter 2, it is important that companies detail which emissions are included in their carbon calculations and which are being excluded. Just as financial statements can be manipulated by moving assets and liabilities around on the balance sheet, carbon metrics will only be as useful as the information on which they are based and the honesty with which they are calculated and reported.

For example, if a company wanted to improve its metrics, it could do so by changing the scope of its carbon footprint and not include certain carbon emissions that should be accounted for. It might decide to "hide" some of the Scope 3 emissions of its footprint in the same way Enron hid a number of its debts off its balance sheet. This is why transparency is paramount and why users of these metrics must understand the ratio limitations to make sure they aren't comparing apples to oranges.

As carbon footprinting becomes more standardized within industries and footprints are done transparently, these metrics will be an increasingly valuable tool for evaluating company performance per carbon emissions against competitors.

Conclusion

As Paul Hawken indicated to us in his ground-breaking book, *The Ecology of Commerce*, and was further expanded upon with Amory and Hunter Lovins, in *Natural Capitalism*, business, environmental, and social interests are components of an integrated harmonious system. A climate strategy rooted in the ROS process incorporates each of these aspects through whole systems thinking. By utilizing the ROS process, activity-based costing, and new carbon equations, decision makers are empowered with quantifiable data to make strategic choices about how to best reduce carbon emissions while improving their brand and saving money - both in times of economic prosperity and uncertainty. By using these three methods together rather than relying on only traditional metrics such as ROI, managers can make holistic, more informed, and better decisions for the short and long-term success of their companies.

SECTION 2

POLICY, REGULATION, & CARBON

Since 2007, a tremendous amount of public policy initiatives concerning carbon emissions have been proposed and passed into law. Business leaders need to keep on top of all these efforts and their effects on company operations. In this section, some of the more recent legislative efforts around climate change are highlighted for leaders to consider when developing mitigation plans.

CHAPTER 5

PUBLIC POLICY

Climate change has been legitimized by scientists, and public officials are taking notice and taking action.[xliv] Although Federal action on GHGs has yet to take place, there has been an explosion in the number of cities, states, and regions taking proactive measures to address climate change through GHG reduction targets, zero-waste goals, and various other strategies.[xlv,xlvi,xlvii] Policy-making groups that formed in the US include the Mayor's Climate Protection Initiative and regional efforts such as:

- The Western Climate Initiative
- The Regional Greenhouse Gas Initiative
- The Midwestern Regional GHG Accord

The CEOs I've talked to are unsure whether to fight or embrace climate legislation, mainly because they are unsure as to how the regulation will shake out. Either way, business leaders need to be educated about the potential implications of climate-change policies on their operations because regulation is gaining momentum and federal action is anticipated by 2010. I have therefore focused this chapter on highlighting the numerous existing and pending climate-related policy measures that businesses need to be aware of and on exploring how businesses can find competitive advantages by incorporating these public policy measures into their climate strategies.

Although these initiatives are piecemeal, they signal a sea change in the public policy of climate change and tell us where we may be headed. The trend of climate change regulations becoming stricter is likely to continue, and it is fair to conclude that carbon emissions will be regulated in the near future. Business ethics expert David Vogel's advice becomes increasingly pertinent: "[companies] must be willing to support public policies that make it easier for them and other firms to do the right thing, and I couldn't agree more."[xlviii]

Why Businesses Should Pay Attention to Climate Policy

> "A concerted, nationwide effort to reduce GHG emissions would almost certainly stimulate economic forces and create business opportunities." — McKinsey 2008[f]

Each new climate policy presents its own set of challenges and opportunities, and companies that stay ahead of regulation will avoid dealing with new laws on an ad hoc basis. This kind of proactive planning will translate into both immediate and future business benefit.

Companies that integrate progressive climate-friendly policies before they are mandated can:

- **Uncover cost savings** through energy efficiency and waste reduction

- **Increase market share** by attracting climate-conscious consumers

- **Earn positive attention** from the media and advocacy groups

- **Motivate their workforce** and enjoy increased employee productivity and reduced hiring costs

No matter what kind of specific policy a business is subject to, the directive is the same: track and reduce GHG emissions. In July 2008, the 8 largest industrial economies (G8) agreed to a 50% cut in GHG emissions by 2050. Additionally, local and state governments are taking significant actions that can potentially have dramatic impacts on where companies locate and how they conduct their business. It is in companies' best interests to take advantage now of the many incentives available to them through their governments and utilities for improving their environmental behavior and avoiding high-cost penalties down the road.

City, State, and Regional Climate Initiatives

A significant amount of the work is being done to make real advances in combating climate change at the local and regional levels.

Cities & States

At the city and local level, much of the action is owed to the Mayors Climate Protection Initiative, a collection of hundreds of cities across the US, representing over 79 million citizens, whose mayors have agreed to meet the Kyoto Protocol locally. These mayors have made a commitment to reduce city GHG emissions to 5% below 1990 levels. Figure 12 shows the distribution of cities that have signed on as of December 2008.[xlix]

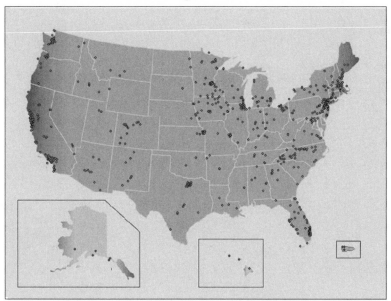

U.S MAYORS CLIMATE PROTECTION AGREEMENT

Figure 12. More than 910 mayors from all 50 states, the District of Columbia, and Puerto Rico have joined the Mayors Climate Protection Initiative. (Map as of Dec. 2008)

Many states are also taking matters into their own hands by setting up climate change commissions, devising action plans, setting GHG performance standards, implementing mandatory or voluntary GHG reporting, and passing climate-change legislation.[1]

Below is a comparative table that highlights the action that states have taken around joining regional initiatives, performing GHG inventories, and developing climate action plans. This table shows us that every single state has begun enacting some type of climate change policy.

State	Regional Initiatives	Climate Action Plan (completed or in progress)	Climate Change Commissions and Advisory Groups	GHG Targets	GHG Inventory	GHG Registry
AK	✓	✓	✓			
AL		✓			✓	✓
AR		✓	✓			
AZ	✓	✓	✓	✓	✓	✓
CA	✓	✓	✓	✓	✓	✓
CO	✓	✓			✓	✓
CT	✓	✓	✓	✓	✓	✓
DC						
DE	✓	✓		✓	✓	✓
FL		✓	✓		✓	✓
GA					✓	✓
HI	✓	✓		✓	✓	✓
IA	✓	✓	✓	✓	✓	✓
ID	✓	✓			✓	✓
IL	✓	✓	✓	✓	✓	✓
IN	✓				✓	
KS	✓				✓	
KY		✓			✓	✓
LA					✓	
MA	✓	✓		✓	✓	✓
MD	✓	✓	✓		✓	✓
ME	✓	✓		✓	✓	✓
MN	✓	✓	✓	✓	✓	✓
MI	✓				✓	✓
MO		✓			✓	✓

State Cont	Regional Initiatives	Climate Action Plan (completed or in progress)	Climate Change Commissions and Advisory Groups	GHG Targets	GHG Inventory	GHG Registry
MS					✓	✓
MT	✓	✓	✓		✓	✓
NC		✓	✓		✓	✓
ND	✓					
NE	✓					
NH	✓	✓		✓	✓	✓
NJ	✓	✓		✓	✓	✓
NM	✓	✓	✓	✓	✓	✓
NV	✓	✓	✓		✓	✓
NY	✓	✓	✓	✓	✓	✓
OH	✓				✓	✓
OK	✓				✓	✓
OR	✓	✓	✓	✓	✓	✓
PA		✓			✓	✓
RI	✓	✓		✓	✓	✓
SC		✓	✓			✓
SD	✓	☐				
TN		✓			✓	✓
TX	✓				✓	✓
UT	✓	✓	✓		✓	✓
VA		✓	✓		✓	✓
VT	✓	✓	✓	✓	✓	✓
WA	✓	✓	✓	✓	✓	✓
WI	✓	✓	✓		✓	✓
WV					✓	✓
WY	✓					✓

State participation around greenhouse gas initiatives.[li]

Regional

As stated at the beginning of the chapter, a number of regional multi-state programs have been put in place to address climate change, including the Western Climate Initiative (WCI), the Regional Greenhouse Gas Initiative (RGGI), and the Midwestern Regional GHG Reduction Accord. All three initiatives detailed below have goals of reducing GHG emissions through cap and trade programs, and in the fall of 2008, RGGI held the first-ever US auction of carbon emission allowances.

This cooperation demonstrates strong political support for comprehensive carbon management policies and should be taken seriously by businesses as an indicator of where Federal climate policy is heading.

These initiatives will have a profound impact on business as the policies and GHG reduction requirements come into effect. Companies will likely have to take action to reduce their emissions even if they are not headquartered in these states, if their suppliers, vendors, customers, retailers, franchises, or shareholders are.

Regional Climate Change Initiative (as of Dec. 2008)	# of States Participating	# of States Observing
Western Climate Initiative	7	6
The Regional Greenhouse Gas Initiative	10	4
Midwestern Regional GHG Reduction Accord	6	3

Regional Initiatives

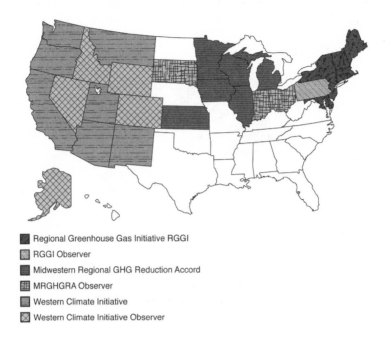

Figure 13. Map of regional climate initiatives in the US. *[lii]*

Other Climate Policies

In addition to the regulations discussed above, states are also taking strong action on a number of additional initiatives. There are too many to cover in one chapter, so I will therefore highlight recent initiatives around vehicle emissions, renewable portfolio standards, waste, green building, commercial building energy codes, and chemical safety.*[liii]*

Vehicle Emissions Standards

Business should pay attention, because many states are considering adapting California's stricter vehicle emission standards requiring a "23% reduction in greenhouse gas emissions from new vehicles by 2012 and a 30% reduction in global warming emissions from new vehicles by 2016."*[liv]*

This type of standard will impact every company's vehicle fleet, from a distributor with thousands of trucks to a small business with one corporate car for its CEO.

Figure 14. So far about 20 states are following California's lead on tough vehicle emissions standards.[lv]

Renewable Portfolio Standards (RPS)

The following table shows the states that have such renewable portfolio standards and the renewable energy requirements as of 2008.

State	Amount	Year	Organization Administering RPS
Arizona	15%	2025	Arizona Corporation Commission
California	20%	2010	California Energy Commission
Colorado	20%	2020	Colorado Public Utilities Commission
Connecticut	23%	2020	Department of Public Utility Control
District of Columbia	11%	2022	DC Public Service Commission
Delaware	20%	2019	Delaware Energy Office
Hawaii	20%	2020	Hawaii Strategic Industries Division
Iowa	105 MW		Iowa Utilities Board
Illinois	25%	2025	Illinois Department of Commerce
Massachusetts	4%	2009	Massachusetts Division of Energy Resources
Maryland	9.5%	2022	Maryland Public Service Commission
Maine	10%	2017	Maine Public Utilities Commission

State Cont'd	Amount	Year	Organization Administering RPS
Minnesota	25%	2025	Minnesota Department of Commerce
Missouri*	11%	2020	Missouri Public Service Commission
Montana	15%	2015	Montana Public Service Commission
New Hampshire	16%	2025	New Hampshire Office of Energy and Planning
New Jersey	22.5%	2021	New Jersey Board of Public Utilities
New Mexico	20%	2020	New Mexico Public Regulation Commission
Nevada	20%	2015	Public Utilities Commission of Nevada
New York	24%	2013	New York Public Service Commission
North Carolina	12.5%	2021	North Carolina Utilities Commission
Oregon	25%	2025	Oregon Energy Office
Pennsylvania	18%	2020	Pennsylvania Public Utility Commission
Rhode Island	15%	2020	Rhode Island Public Utilities Commission
Texas	5,880 MW	2015	Public Utility Commission of Texas
Utah*	20%	2025	Utah Department of Environmental Quality
Vermont*	10%	2013	Vermont Department of Public Service
Virginia*	12%	2022	Virginia Department of Mines, Minerals, and Energy
Washington	15%	2020	Washington Secretary of State
Wisconsin	10%	2015	Public Service Commission of Wisconsin

Summary of states with renewable portfolio standards.[lvi]

* Missouri, Virginia, and Vermont set voluntary goals instead of adopting RPS standards with binding targets.

Zero Waste Goals

As of 2008, at least nine US states have less than five years of landfill capacity.[lvii] Combined with rising consumption and populations, this has forced many US cities to export their waste at considerable cost, which gets passed down to consumers and business in the form of higher disposal costs. For example, six days a week, Seattle sends a 100-car train loaded with the city's municipal waste to a landfill 300 miles away in Oregon. It is extremely expensive, and as cities' budgets are being squeezed all over the country, many municipalities are looking for ways to reduce their waste and its associated costs. This means that these costs will be passed along to consumers, with businesses bearing the brunt of these costs as the largest producers of waste.

Increasing costs will dramatically affect how companies do business in these cities because they will be forced to respond by reducing, minimizing, or eliminating waste from their operations, products, and services—especially in the industries that are the top 10 leaders in disposal waste, including.[lviii]

- Metal mining

- Electric utilities

- Primary metals

- Chemicals

- Hazardous waste/solvent recovery

- Paper

- Food

- Transportation equipment

- Plastics

Moreover, these waste-disposal issues will impact where companies locate and will have a major impact both up and down companies' supply chains. Companies that prepare for these policies and eliminate waste in their operations will be at a competitive and financial advantage in cities with strong waste-reduction goals and incentives, including the following that have announced zero waste goals:

- San Francisco, CA
- Seattle, WA
- Oakland, CA
- Minneapolis, MN
- Berkeley, CA
- Boulder, CO
- Carrboro, NC
- Summit County, CO
- Matanuska-Susitna Borough, AK

Green Building Requirements

Buildings in the US use a tremendous amount of resources including electricity, water, and energy. More communities and cities are recognizing the impact that buildings have and are mandating green building requirements. Currently, Federal, state, and local green building programs require only government-owned, funded, or sponsored buildings to adhere to green standards. Although no programs are mandatory for corporate buildings, this may begin to change, as some municipalities such as King County, Washington, where Seattle is located, are now looking to require the GHG emissions of new buildings to be tracked and reported as part of the permitting process. For corporate buildings, many incentives exist for green building efforts such as expedited permitting and plan reviews, and tax credits that help offset any additional costs of constructing the building "green."

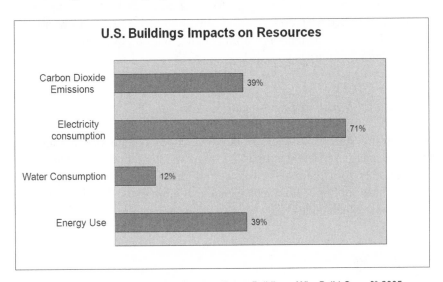

Source: U.S. Environmental Protection Agency, "Green Buildings: Why Build Green?" 2005.

Figure 15. Resources used by US buildings

Through an informal search conducted in 2006, I found that only eight US jurisdictions had mandatory green building requirements for private-sector commercial buildings:

- Austin, TX

- Battery Park, NY

- Frisco, TX

- Seattle, WA

- Novato, CA

- Santa Cruz, CA

- Telluride, CO

- Sebastopol, CA

Two years later, approximately 38 states had incorporated the American Society of Heating, Refrigerating and Air-Conditioning Engineers (ASHRAE) codes and/or International Energy Conservation Codes (IECC) into mandatory building codes within government buildings or commercial buildings statewide.

Commercial Building Energy Codes

In some states, commercial building codes dictate that a minimum level of energy efficiency must be met and that buildings must meet requirements for "thermal resistance" of their shell and windows, with heating and cooling equipment efficiency minimums. All but 13 states have adopted such codes.[lix]

Chemical Safety

In the US, it is currently up to the Environmental Protection Agency (EPA) to declare a chemical unsafe for consumer use. However, a number of voluntary industry initiatives have recently popped up that follow the European model, in which companies have to actually prove their chemical's safety before it can be distributed to consumers. One set of regulations in Europe is the REACH (Registration, Evaluation and Authorization of Chemicals) accords. Developed by the European

Chemicals Bureau (ECB) and entered into force in June 2007, REACH is based on the idea that it is up to the manufacturer to ensure that the chemicals it makes and puts on the market in the EU do not adversely affect human health or the environment prior to being sold.[ix] Chemical use and safety is just one more area in which companies will increasingly be expected to raise their level of responsibility in order to reduce waste and create a healthier planet.

Conclusion

This list of public policy actions should make business leaders take notice. Even if a company is not located in one of the cities or states where these policies are in effect currently, you can bet that it has stakeholders (suppliers, customers, investors, etc) that are. States, municipalities, and utilities are offering a number of incentives for taking action, so by starting to act now and taking advantage of incentives, companies can lower their up-front costs, reduce payback periods, and gain a competitive advantage in anticipation of future regulation.

CHAPTER 6

CARBON TAXES & CAP AND TRADE

Many companies are concerned in this economic environment and there are three things businesses do not like: uncertainty, regulation, and taxes. They are worried about climate regulation and are asking "Will we be taxed?" and "If so, how?" Just as businesses typically steadfastly resist any new tax, there will be no exception for either a carbon tax or a cap-and-trade regimen. This is especially true of companies in the extractive, automotive, transportation, and manufacturing industries because they are the biggest emitters of GHGs and therefore would be the most at risk with either a cap-and-trade system or a carbon tax. While the discussion at the national and regional levels is focused on cap and trade, at the more local level of cities and municipalities, carbon taxes are being considered and passed.

This chapter explains what carbon taxes and cap-and-trade systems are being considered, how they are being enacted, and their implications for business. Business leaders may find that smart climate policy could end up being smart regulatory and tax policy as well.

Why a Carbon Tax?

While the current national and political mood is more focused on tax cuts, supporters of carbon taxation believe that this is the easiest and most straight forward approach to regulating carbon emissions, and that a carbon tax would be relatively easy to administer.

The residents of Boulder, Colorado, favored a carbon tax to meet their carbon-reduction goal and to also provide a long-term revenue source to fund their climate program.[lxi] New York City Mayor Michael Bloomberg is also a supporter of carbon tax, but instead of a local tax, he has called for a national carbon tax, which he believes would slow global warming, promote low-carbon economic growth, increase innovation, and provide some certainty to the market about carbon regulation at the same time.[lxii]

At the international level, Sweden has a carbon tax, and both Canada (Quebec and British Columbia) and France are beginning to address provincial and national concerns over GHG emissions and climate change through the support of carbon taxes. Quebec has made a pledge to cut emissions by 6% from 1990 levels by 2012, some of which will be encouraged through taxation. British Columbia has a goal of 33% reduction by 2020. France's recent support for carbon taxes comes from French President Sarkozy's strong desire to aggressively reduce GHG emissions through both a national carbon tax on global-warming pollutants and a European levy on imports from countries not complying with the Kyoto Protocol.

How Carbon Taxes Are Being Implemented

How carbon taxation will impact businesses, industries, and individuals across the country is a key question. How it is implemented could vary and have far different consequences for different industries. One way a tax could be implemented would be based on the "polluter pays" principle, in which the company directly responsible for emissions would pay the tax. This would hit fossil-fuel consuming industries such as cement manufacturing, mining, and energy production the hardest because they have the most direct emissions, whereas service-based and retail businesses would be impacted much less because the majority of their emissions are indirect and are tied to the manufacturing, energy, and transportation of their goods and services.

Another way the tax could be administered would be to collect carbon taxes where fossil fuels enter the economy, such as ports, oil refineries, natural-gas providers, and coal-processing plants. According to the Congressional Budget Office, "applying the levy to as few as 2,000 entities could reach nearly all the fossil fuel consumed in the US economy and would cover 82 percent of US greenhouse gas emissions."[lxiii] By setting a tax rate on the production of carbon in any form, industries would be encouraged to emit less from a purely financial perspective.

A third way the tax could be administered might follow what Boulder, Colorado did in 2006, when it decided to charge businesses and residents a fee on their city bills based on electricity usage by square footage. According to the city council's research on rate structures, the rates varied depending on how much each sector contributed to the total collected revenue, with the commercial sector contributing the most, at 53% of total emissions, residential at 27% and the industrial sector at 19%.[lxiv]

Boulder's Rate Structures Depending on Each Sector's Contribution to the Total Collected Revenue[lxv]

	Residential	Commercial	Industrial
Percent of Total Emissions (2005)	27	53	19
Percent of Total Reductions	31	41	22
Percent of Total Private Investment	19	76	5
Percent of Public Investment	58	39	3

Under Boulder's system, the tax rates will be reviewed and changed annually. The tax will generate about $1 million for the city annually through 2012, to help the community reach its goal for reducing carbon emissions by 350,000 metric tons. Tax policy similar to that in Boulder will cause commercial businesses to pay an average of an extra $37 a year and industrial customers to pay $2,832 annually based on their consumption of electricity.[lxvi] If the Boulder model were adopted nationally, it would disproportionately affect industrial businesses, and all companies and consumers could expect the additional costs to be passed down.

Quebec, Canada, took a different approach by taxing all hydrocarbons related to energy generation used in the province, from coal to heating oil.[lxvii] The tax varied according to the amount of carbon dioxide produced from each fuel source and affected various businesses differently.[lxviii]

ENERGY TYPE	TAX PER UNIT
Gasoline	0.21¢ per gallon
Diesel	0.23¢ per gallon
Light heating oil	0.25¢ per gallon
Heavy heating oil	0.26¢ per gallon
Coke used in steel making	0.39¢
Propane	0.13¢ per gallon
Coal	$8 per ton

Figure 16. Carbon tax rates in Quebec, Canada.[lxix]

British Columbia, Canada, introduced a different type of carbon tax that went into effect July 1, 2008, on most fossil fuels, including gasoline, diesel, natural gas, coal, propane, and home heating fuel. This tax will begin at a low rate based on $10 per ton of carbon emissions, increasing by $5 a year to $30 per ton in 2012, to reflect the true cost to be paid for generating GHG. This will mean the tax on gasoline will be an extra 9.1 cents per gallon in 2008, rising to 27.3 cents in 2012.[lxx]

It is expected that industry will pay up to 70% of the new carbon taxes. What is different about British Columbia's carbon tax is that it will be revenue neutral, and no money raised will go toward program spending. Instead, the carbon tax revenue, which is estimated to reach $1.8 billion over three years, will be returned to businesses through other tax cuts, encouraging businesses to use the money to adopt greener practices.[lxxi] According to British Columbia's Finance Minister, Carole Taylor, the carbon tax is one of the government's key building blocks to help it reach its legislated goal of reducing British Columbia's GHG emissions by 33 percent by 2020.[lxxii]

A carbon tax may be one of the simplest methods for municipalities to monitor, control and affect GHG reductions. As citizens and consumers demand climate action, business must anticipate that potential carbon taxes may be coming down the pike and prepare to respond. In this pending regulatory environment, a smart climate policy is not only smart business management, but also potentially prudent tax policy. That being said, new taxes in this political and economic environment are still difficult for many politicians to get behind.

Cap and Trade

As of early 2009, a federal cap and trade system was not in place in the U.S. Although the Warner-Lieberman climate bill which proposed a federal cap and trade system was voted down in the Senate in June 2008, President Obama has stated publicly that he intends for the US to once again take a lead on climate change and has expressed a preference for a federal cap and trade market as the best means do this.

> "By putting a price on carbon, a cap-and-trade market would allow firms with a comparative advantage in carbon-saving technology to increase profits by emitting less carbon and selling their permits on the open market, providing continual incentives to develop better technologies at real economic gains." —Maria Damon, Economics Professor, University of Washington[g]

Business leaders need to understand the cap-and-trade system and plan for ways to take advantage of this new market opportunity.

What is a Cap-and-Trade System?

A market-based cap-and-trade system, unlike a legislated carbon tax, draws on the power of the marketplace to reduce emissions by using supply and demand. In practice, a cap-and-trade system creates a financial incentive for companies to reduce their GHG emissions by assigning a cost to those GHG emissions. First, a cap is established by either a regulator or a market entity to limit emissions across all businesses or from a designated group of emitters such as power plants or manufacturing facilities. The emissions allowed under this cap are then divided up into individual allowances—usually equal to one metric ton of CO_2 equivalent—that allows the company the right to emit that amount of pollution annually. The cap is set lower than current emissions in order to encourage emission reduction.

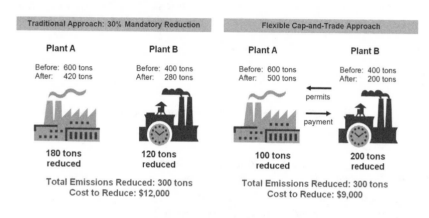

Figure 17. Illustration of how a cap-and-trade market reduces emission at a lower cost.[lxxiii]

To reduce total emissions, the cap must be lowered over time, or some allotment of allowances must be permanently retired. This means that the price for the remaining allowances will increase. In the system where the cap is lowered, the governing authority lowers the cap by some percentage, as is the case in the Chicago Climate Exchange (CCX), where members voluntarily enter a binding agreement and the cap is lowered by a certain percentage annually. In the other system, emission allowances are permanently retired so they cannot be used the next year, which reduces the total number of allowances available for companies to use or purchase. This has the effect of reducing emissions overall and increasing the price for the remaining allowances, making it more expensive to practice business as usual. This system relies on market price to encourage companies to reduce GHG emissions.

An efficient and effective cap and trade system consists of several key components, noted in the table on the next page.

COMPONENT	DEFINITION
Emissions Cap	A limit on the total amount of pollution that can be emitted from all regulated sources
Allowance	An authorization to emit a fixed amount of a pollutant
Measurement	Accurate tracking of all emissions
Flexibility	Sources can choose how to reduce emissions, including whether to buy additional allowances from other sources that reduce emissions
Allowance Trading	Sources can buy or sell allowances on the open market. Because the total number of allowances is limited by the cap, emission reductions are ensured
Compliance	At the end of each compliance period, each source must own at least as many allowances as it has emissions

Why This Mechanism?

A cap-and-trade mechanism restricts the amount of GHG emissions allowed and assigns a dollar figure to each unit of CO_2 equivalent. Emissions, as represented by individual allowance, take on a financial value. A key advantage of a cap-and-trade system is that it sets a clear limit on overall emissions but gives companies flexibility in the manner in which they may achieve their emission targets.

Companies can choose to make internal emission reductions or to buy and sell their allowances and continue operating in the most profitable manner available to them. Those that are able to reduce emissions internally can make money by selling their extra allowances to companies that want or need to purchase them. Then, as the price of a unit of CO_2 equivalent goes up, the emission allowances become more valuable to those that can sell them and more costly to those who need to purchase them.

What Cap-and-Trade Means for Business

Companies that proactively address climate change and prepare for a cap-and-trade system can reap multiple benefits by staying ahead of regulation and reducing their climate liability. Companies that do so may find cost savings and even new revenue streams through the trading market. As stated earlier, the four key benefits are:

Stay Ahead of Regulation: Companies should consider getting ahead of regulation by conducting a carbon footprint and developing systems to record, track, and reduce their carbon emissions. A carbon footprint gives companies more self knowledge about the extent to which they may be at risk from their emissions and how much they may need to change their practices or pay.

Cost Savings: Currently, many utility incentives and companies may be able to take advantage of existing incentives, mainly around energy efficiency, to lower implementation costs before a Federal or regional mandate occurs and these incentives disappear.

New Revenue Streams: Businesses that are able to reduce their emissions below established caps have the opportunity to develop additional revenue streams through the sale of allowances under the trade mechanism. They will also be able to sell their reductions immediately or to hold them and save them for future use or sale.

Climate Liability: There is no longer much of a question as to whether companies will pay for emissions; it is only a question of when and how much. There will be GHG regulations, and there will be a cost of compliance for emitting GHGs. Companies that do not assess and address their climate risk will be liable and also less well prepared to participate and prosper in a cap-and-trade regime.

Follow the SO_2 Market Example

The world's first cap-and-trade system was developed in the United States in 1990 through amendments to the Clean Air Act. The intent of this system was to reduce emissions of sulfur dioxide (SO_2), the primary cause of acid rain. This proved to be both an environmental and economic success. By the end of the 1990s, US power plants had reduced their SO_2 emissions to a surprising level of 22% below the mandated reductions. And these dramatic reductions were achieved at a fraction of the projected costs.lxxiv

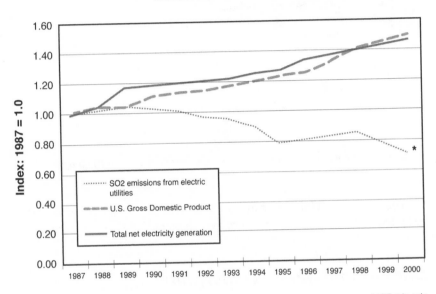

Relationship of U.S. GDP to Electricity Generation and SO_2 Emissions from 1987 to 2000

Source: EPA, DOC, DOE, respectively

* ARP units only

Figure 18. Relationship of US GDP to electricity generation and SO_2 emissions from 1987 to 2000.[lxxv]

In fact, George W. Bush *further* lowered the cap on SO_2 by *an additional* 40% with no significant outcry from the business community.[lxxvi] The system worked because it was based on market mechanisms that created incentives that businesses could understand and plan for.

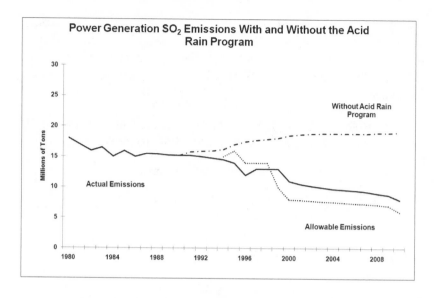

Figure 19. Reductions in SO_2 emissions as a result of the acid rain program.
lxxvii

The European Union borrowed directly from this model to design its projected CO_2 cap-and-trade system, which went into effect in early 2007.

The Carbon Market Opportunity

The three most well known GHG trading systems are: the Chicago Climate Exchange (CCX), the EU Trading Scheme (EU ETS) and the New South Wales Greenhouse Gas Abatement Scheme (GGAS). The CCX was largely established by a few individuals who believed that because the US hadn't signed the Kyoto Protocol that some kind of mechanism was needed to encourage businesses to efficiently and effectively participate in a market that would help them reduce their carbon output and offer financial gain at the same time.

The CCX began trading in 2003 and is currently the only global trading exchange for all greenhouse gases. Emitters that join the exchange, including companies, utilities, and public-sector entities, voluntarily enter into legally binding contracts to reduce their emissions to at least 6% below their emissions baseline by 2010, based on the organization's average annual emissions between 1998 and 2001. Those that reduce even further below the target may sell their surplus emission allowances, and those that fail to meet their reduction commitments must buy allowances to stay in compliance. Emissions offsets can also be generated through exchange-certified projects located throughout the world.

Although the price of carbon hovered below $2 per metric ton on the CCX at the end of 2008, the costs are expected to fluctuate and increase. Realizing that carbon trading represents the future, and with the first carbon allowances auctioned off by RGGI, over 350 organizations have joined CCX, including those in the table below:

INDUSTRY SECTOR	COMPANIES
Auto	Ford Motor Company
Chemicals	DuPont Dow Corning; Potash Corp; Rhodia Energy Brasil Ltda
Coal Mining	PinnOak Resources, LLC; Jim Walter Resources, Inc.
Counties	Miami-Dade County, FL; Sacramento County, CA; King County, WA
Electric Power Generation	Alliant Energy; American Electric Power; Puget Sound Energy; TECO Energy, Inc.
Financial Institutions	Bank of America
Municipalities	Boulder, CO; Chicago, IL; Oakland, CA; Portland, OR; Aspen, CO
Technology	IBM; Intel Corporation; STMicroelectronics; Freescale Semiconductor

European Climate Exchange

The EU ETS supported by Kyoto, is the largest organization of its kind in the world. It includes more than 11,500 facilities including coke ovens, coal plants, cement factories and iron works across the EU's 27 member nations. The first phase of trading began in 2005 and covered only CO_2, but the second phase which began in 2008 allows member states to opt-in to expand their scope to include other greenhouse gasses. Market driven CO_2 was selling at about 22 Euros per metric ton as of December 2008. The European Climate Exchange (ECX), an offshoot of CCX, holds more than 80% of the exchange-traded volume in the European market.[lxxviii]

New South Wales GGAS

This Australian market was created in 2003. The GGAS imposes mandatory GHG benchmarks on all electricity retailers and certain other parties in New South Wales to abate the emission of greenhouse gases from electricity consumption. The state capped its overall emissions at just over seven metric tons of CO_2 equivalent emissions annually. By 2006, "twenty-eight out of thirty-five participants fully met their abatement obligations, while the other seven were allowed to carry forward their shortfalls into 2007."[lxxix]

Other Market Mechanisms

Clean Development Mechanism (CDM)

The CDM is an incentive for developing countries to reduce their emissions without caps through what are called certified emission reduction (CER) projects. CERs are essentially carbon allowances—each unit equals the reduction of one metric ton of CO_2 or its equivalent. Through CDM, industrialized nations earn CERs by partnering with developing nations that agree to host CDM-registered, third-party verified emissions-reductions projects. As of 2008, there were over 3,000 projects in the CDM pipeline, 1108 of which are registered. The CDM anticipates that these projects will yield an overall reduction of 2.7 billion tons of CO_2 by 2012.[lxxx] The United Nations Framework Convention on Climate Change (UNFCCC) recently launched a website to encourage greater CDM trading.

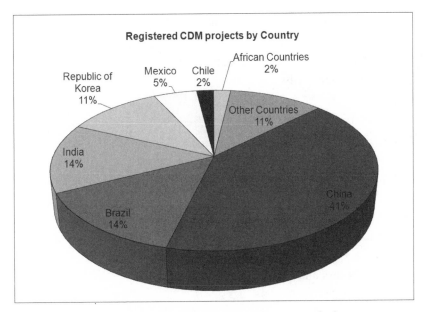

Figure 20. Registered CDM projects by country. [lxxxi]

Ecosystem Marketplaces

In addition to carbon, other ecosystem markets have emerged. The below chart highlights the other markets, their scope, and potential market size.[lxxxii] The numbers provided below are the lowest, most conservative estimates per market.

	Projected Market Size ($ in Billions)			
Other Ecosystem Markets *(In dollars per year)*	Current	2010	2020	2050
Water Quality: - Compliant Water Trading -Voluntary Watershed Mgmt - Government Watershed PDEs	$5.22	$5.22*	$9	$32

Other Markets Cont'd	Current	2010	2020	2050
Biodiversity: - Compliant Biodiversity Offsets - Voluntary Biodiversity Offsets - Government Mandated Biodiversity PE - Individual Fisheries Quotas (ITQs & IFQs) - Recreation - Genetic Resources(Access and Benefit Sharing)	**$16.43**	**$18.88**	**$42.2**	**$85.9**
Land Conservation: - Land Conservation - Tradable Development Rights - Certified Forest Products - Certified Agricultural Products	**$55**	**$127**	**$230**	**$950**

* Projection unavailable, 2008 numbers used.

Joint Implementation

Another Kyoto mechanism similar to the CDM is joint implementation. Instead of projects taking place in developing nations, these emission-reduction projects are created in industrialized nations. According to the UNFCCC, Russia dominates this market, with more than 80% of the estimated annual emissions reductions for 2006, the most recent year of complete data at the time of this writing.

World Green Exchange

The World Green Exchange launched in February 2008 to serve the growing market for trading renewable energy and environmental commodities. Focusing on green power, renewable energy certificates (RECs), voluntary emission reductions (VERs), and GHG emissions credits, the World Green Exchange is a global marketplace with a focus on the US.

Conclusion

Regardless of the mechanism, a price on carbon is looming and businesses need to be prepared. A carbon tax system may be easier to administer and simpler for companies to understand, because they simply can write a check for any emissions exceeding a certain threshold. However, the major drawback of a tax system is that although it guarantees a market price it does *not* guarantee the degree to which the environment will benefit. Some companies might find it easier to pay the tax instead of reducing emissions, and in those instances it becomes much more difficult to reduce emissions nationally. Taxes can also be a political lightening rod and too often are subject to the party in power. They are also less palatable to businesses than other market mechanisms. In light of these realities a cap-and-trade market may be the best solution in the US.

Therefore, although federal legislation was still lacking as recently as early 2009, nearly three quarters of US states are involved in developing regional cap and trade systems, and it won't be long before this forces the Federal government to develop a national standard. This will bring new regulation and place limits on the amount of emissions for individual businesses but it will also open up a new revenue stream for companies that take action and can realize reductions.

Businesses that reduce their emissions will realize the dual benefit of savings from lower energy costs, and lower carbon costs when either a tax or cap-and-trade program comes into play. Conversely, those that fail to take action will likely experience both higher energy costs and higher costs associated with GHG emissions. Companies should baseline their emissions today so they are prepared to take advantage of the system, however it unfolds. Smart business leaders will develop strategies that not only reduce their carbon footprint but also open new revenue opportunities through cap and trade.

SECTION 3

THE MARKET: DEMANDING ACTION

The market is not waiting for politicians; it is already taking action. Industries varying from insurance to finance are getting involved, energy prices are volatile and soaring, customers are demanding action, and businesses throughout the supply chain are being asked about their climate policies and plans for emissions reduction. The following chapters underscore the importance of taking action on climate now because the market is increasingly demanding it.

CHAPTER 7

ENERGY

Our country's era of abundant, cheap fossil fuel energy is coming to an end. For more than a century—with the exception of the energy crisis of the 1970s—our economy has been able to thrive off this low-cost energy. This is all rapidly changing, and companies are now in a position where they must adapt to new realities:

- Increasing energy prices

- Business risk due to energy uncertainty and volatility

- Potential regulation of GHGs as they pertain to energy use

- Cost-competitive renewable energy opportunities

How can businesses prepare for both a new energy paradigm and the uncertain impacts of climate change? In this chapter, I explain what this new energy reality is, what it means for business, and what companies are already doing to address it.

> "As energy costs continue to rise and power grid capacity is pushed to the brink, energy provisioning and consumption are emerging as critical concerns for today's companies." —Paul Goetz, EMC Vice President of Consulting and Management Services[h]

The New Energy Reality

Increased Price Volatility

From 1999 to 2007 we witnessed the prices of coal, natural gas, and oil skyrocket. According to the Energy Information Administration (EIA), energy prices for these three fossil fuels - which make up roughly 70% of our country's energy mix have increased between 200% - 300% over those eight years.[lxxxiii] The increase in the price of oil may even be on the conservative side, because its price has increased at an even more dramatic rate in recent times; including for example the price of oil shot up $25 a barrel on a single day on September 22, 2008.[lxxxiv]

Of course, we've seen oil prices come down since then, fueled in large part by the worldwide financial crisis. When the idea for this book first germinated back in February 2008, the cost of a barrel of oil had just topped $100 for the first time. It hit $148 in July 2008, but then sank back to below $40 in December. This being said, oil prices are extremely volatile and many analysts predict it to be back over $100 a barrel by 2010.[lxxxv]

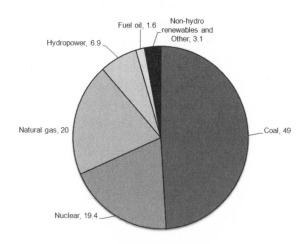

Current National Fuel Mix

Fuel oil, 1.6
Non-hydro renewables and Other, 3.1
Hydropower, 6.9
Natural gas, 20
Coal, 49
Nuclear, 19.4

Source: US Department of Energy, EIA, 2007 data

Figure 21. Current US fuel mix.

This volatility has major implications for businesses, especially for industries like the airlines that traditionally try to hedge against major price fluctuations. When oil prices increased dramatically at the beginning of the year, all the big domestic air carriers except Southwest lost millions because they were not protected by longer term fuel contracts that hedged against fuel price increases. Fearing even greater prices, they then signed onto longer-term contracts which cause them to be burned a second time when oil prices tumbled in October 2008.

The take home message is that companies will no longer be able to depend on cheap carbon-based energy going forward, as volatility increasingly defines the market.

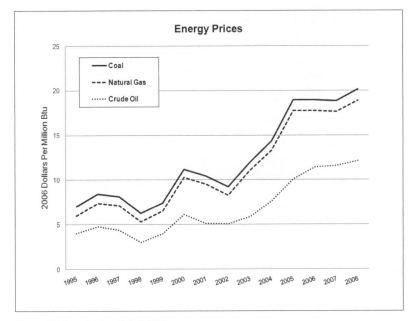

Source: EIA Annual Energy Outlook 2008

Figure 22. Historic energy prices, 1995 to 2008.

The causes of these price fluctuations are many and are difficult to decipher, but it is easy to see how decreases in supply and increases in demand are direct contributors.

Peak Oil

Shell's CEO, Jeroen van der Veer, has estimated that "after 2015, the supply of easy-to-access oil will no longer keep up with demand."[lxxxvi] His assessment is in lock-step with Exxon-Mobil's own projections, which show that we either already have or will soon reach a global state of "peak oil," which is the moment when the world demand permanently outstrips supply. In fact, some studies show that 54 of the 65 largest oil-producing countries have *already* passed their peak oil production—the US included.[lxxxvii]

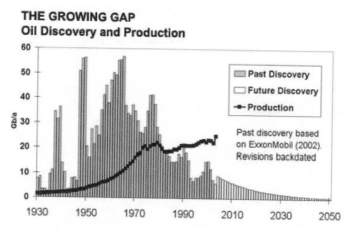

Figure 23. Oil discovery and production.[lxxxviii]

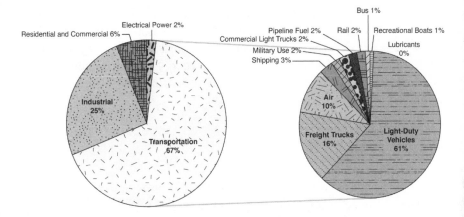

Transportation Uses More Than 2/3 of Oil in the U.S.

2004 U.S. Fuel Consumption by Sector

Source: EIA, Annual Energy Outlook 2007 with Projections to 2030. Tables 2 and 7. http://www.eia.doe.gov

Figure 24. 2004 US fuel consumption by sector.

Meanwhile as the global supply of oil diminishes, countries like China and India are greatly expanding their use of oil. Global population is expected to increase by 50% by 2050, and developing countries are striving to attain the American standard of living. The regions of the world that still have large oil reserves—including the Middle East, Venezuela, Nigeria, Sudan, and Russia—are politically unstable. When these factors are combined with the unpredictability and strain on energy supply that is already taking place, it is plain to see that energy supplies are only going to get worse and prices are likely only to increase.

"The drivers moving our economy away from fossil fuels and toward clean energy and sustainable technologies are inexorable. Fossil fuel prices are volatile and climbing, while a steady stream of exciting new alternatives reach into the mass market. And climate, national security, and supply concerns are converging to accelerate policy changes that will fundamentally realign long-term energy markets." —Rhys Roth, Climate Solutions, Director of Clean Energy Programs[i]

What this Means for Business

Businesses will have to plan for and react to a wide variety of issues related to the new energy landscape. A few areas businesses should be particularly aware of include higher energy costs, a tightening regulatory environment around climate change, new energy pricing systems due to growing demand during peak hours, and uncertainty associated with new technologies such as carbon sequestration.

Higher Costs

Higher energy costs have effects that ripple through every aspect of a business, ultimately impacting the bottom line in a variety of ways. Raw materials, manufacturing, transportation, the distribution of goods and services, business travel, and commuting are just a few of the things that come at a higher price when the cost of energy goes up.

Higher energy prices don't affect only the immediate cost of doing business; they also wreak havoc on long-term budget projections. Unpredictable price fluctuations make it difficult for businesses to project and prepare monthly, quarterly, and annual budgets and financials. Recall what happened to California businesses during the energy crisis and the rolling blackouts of 2001 or the changes we've seen in the airline industry of late. Ten US airlines went out of business in a single month in the spring of 2008, including Eos, Aloha Airlines, SkyBus, Champion, and Air Midwest; the latter three all stated that recent volatility and increases in fuel costs were the primary cause.[lxxxix]

GHG Regulation

Another major reason that business leaders can expect fossil fuel prices to increase is the additional costs imposed through upcoming GHG regulation. Below is a breakdown of GHG emission by business sector. Almost 49% of total global emissions come from electricity, heat, and transportation, all of which are universal business needs. Utilities looking to reduce their emissions will likely pass along the costs of doing so to businesses and consumers.

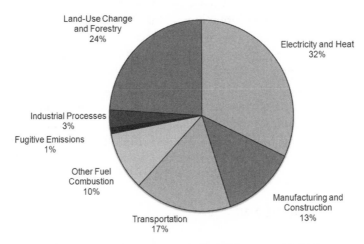

Source: WRI Climate Analysis Indicators Tool, version 3.0. Washington, DC, WRI, 2006

Figure 25. Global CO$_2$ emissions by sector, 2000.

Peak Load, Growing Demand

The emergence of "peak load" pricing will also impact the cost of energy for businesses. Peak load is a policy of raising prices when the demand for service is at its highest, typically during business hours. This relatively new policy means that where a flat fee per kWh was once charged, businesses will be hit with a stiffer bill for energy use when demand is highest- heating in the winter, and air conditioning in the summer. This will also impact business because energy demand is usually highest during traditional "business hours."

Potential Cost of Carbon Capture and Sequestration (CCS)

Carbon sequestration is a young technology that is not yet ready for implementation, but two basic business questions that need to be answered are "When will this be required?" and "What will the additional costs be?"[xc]

Carbon sequestration is the process of capturing the carbon during the energy generation process and then pumping the CO_2 underground to be stored in deep geologic formations. This has gained prominence and become a major topic lately for GHG intensive industries such as coal, oil, and natural gas. CCS was the hot topic at the National Governor's Association meeting in 2008 and is important to business because not only will consumers, businesses, and taxpayers likely have to pay the additional cost of the carbon capture and sequestration, but it is uncertain at this time which types of businesses will be required to do so, where the carbon will be sequestered, and how it will be transported across the country. That being said, there will be a ton of money to be made when it is decided.

Business Solutions

The two most important things businesses can do to insulate themselves against energy price increases, new climate regulations, and volatility is to make investments in energy efficiency and to purchase renewable energy. According to the Northwest Power and Conservation Council, energy efficiency is the cheapest source of new power both for business and utilities.[xci]

Energy Efficiency

Energy efficiency improvements are not only about saving energy and reducing GHG emissions but also saving money. Simply put, in an uncertain economy, energy efficiency is a must-do for business leaders.

Moreover, as the cost of providing energy has increased over the past decade, numerous utilities across the country have rolled out energy efficiency incentives to help firms be smarter and use less electricity and heat. This not only reduces the up-front cost of improvements but also shortens the payback period, and, once this payback is met, it is a net positive to the bottom line over its lifetime.

Following are some examples of companies that have found cost savings through energy efficiency.

Fred Hutchison Cancer Research Center[xcii]

The Fred Hutchison Cancer Research Center instituted 25 projects and took advantage of multiple local and Federal energy efficiency incentives that in many cases reduced the payback period and up-front costs of the projects. These projects required virtually no employee action or change in company culture.[xciii] For example, the center installed off-hour lighting, fan shutoffs, occupancy sensors, high-efficiency chillers, LED exit signs, heat recovery from washers, night setbacks for temperature, and water-conservation devices.

FINANCIAL	BRAND	SUSTAINABILITY
Saves $317,000 annually	Employees are motivated by this environmental commitment	Saves energy equivalent to powering 1,200 homes annually

Staples Seattle[xciv]

Staples installed energy management systems, efficient HVAC systems, and LED exit signs with an initial investment of $3.1 million, or the equivalent of 91¢ per square foot.

FINANCIAL	BRAND	SUSTAINABILITY
Saves $985,000 annually. IRR of 29%	Employees enjoyed better lighting and realized increased productivity	Saves energy equivalent to powering 3,700 homes annually

Pfizer[xcv]

Pfizer requires all its manufacturing, research and development, large logistic facilities, and large offices to annually report their total annual energy use, conduct periodic energy audits to identify their energy conservation opportunities, and identify and prioritize these targets and actions.

FINANCIAL	BRAND	SUSTAINABILITY
Invested $70 million from 2002 to 2005 and realized a net savings of $30 million	Undeclared by the company	Decreased absolute CO_2 emissions by 4%, or roughly 201,000 metric tons of CO_2

Standing Stone Brewing Company

This small brewery took advantage of numerous Oregon business tax credits to make energy efficiency improvements. It invested in a variable-speed hood-control system environmental management system, and improved lighting.

FINANCIAL	BRAND	SUSTAINABILITY
Saved roughly $2,100 annually. Reduced its payback from 6.5 years to 3.2 years	Helped the company be seen as a leading environmental brewery	GHG emission reduced because of lower energy usage. Exact numbers not disclosed

Renewables for Stability

One bright star within this energy discussion is that the costs of renewable energy have decreased because of increased demand, economies of scale, and innovations throughout the clean technology sector. These cost reductions have enabled many major companies that want to do something about both climate change and energy-price stability to either invest in on-site renewable power generation or purchase renewable power from their utilities. Companies such as Wal-Mart, Google, Staples, and REI have all recently made moves to increase the amount of renewable energy they use. According to Kevin Hagen, Director of Corporate Social Responsibility for REI, the corporation found that purchasing a portion of its energy from renewable sources was an effective way to decrease price volatility and actually saved the company money as energy prices increased during 2007 & 2008.[xcvi]

The World Resources Institute has teamed up with 12 leading corporations to create the Green Power Market Development Group, whose goal is to build corporate markets for 1000 megawatts of new, cost-competitive green power by 2010.[xcvii] A few corporate partners include Alcoa, Inc.; Dow; DuPont; FedEx; General Motors; Google, Inc.; IBM; and Starbucks.

Companies Purchasing Renewable Power

As stated earlier, with the cost of traditional fossil fuels trending upward, purchasing fixed-cost renewable power can become an effective cost-containment strategy. Although renewable energy is still more expensive in some markets, it is not subject to the price spikes or peak demand surcharges of fossil fuels. The three examples discussed below focus on the benefits of purchasing renewable energy.

Intel Corp. [xcviii]

Intel Corp. purchases 1.3 billion kWh of green energy annually.

FINANCIAL	BRAND	SUSTAINABILITY
Undeclared by company	They are now known as the biggest corporate buyer of renewable energy, and No. 1 spot on EPA's Fortune 500 Green Power Partners list	The EPA estimates that this purchase would power more than 130,000 avg. American homes and is the equivalent to taking more than 185,000 passenger cars off the road each year

PepsiCo [xcix]

PepsiCo's three-year purchase comprises more than 1 billion kWh annually, offsetting 100% of its electricity use.

FINANCIAL	BRAND	SUSTAINABILITY
Undeclared by company	Received No. 2 spot on EPA's Fortune 500 Green Power Partners list	EPA estimates PepsiCo's purchase is the same amount of electricity needed to power nearly 90,000 average American homes annually

REI

REI purchased 20% of its energy from renewable power and realized the following benefits since the program's inception:[c]

FINANCIAL	BRAND	SUSTAINABILITY
Saved $100K by purchasing 25% of its power from renewable sources	This is the type of action its customers and employees would expect.	Dropped CO_2 emissions from electricity by 1/3

Conclusion

Businesses need to realize that there is a new reality when it comes to energy. In this country, the cost of fossil fuels will continue to increase as supply becomes more uncertain, volatile, and subject to new carbon regulation. In today's economy, businesses need to prepare and adapt to be more efficient with their energy use and look toward renewable sources of power whenever possible to provide some cost savings and certainty to their bottom lines. Additionally, although a number of Federal, state, and utility incentives exist right now to help companies offset some of the up-front costs of making these changes, if and when sweeping climate legislation is passed the funding for these incentives is expected to dry up. Companies that take advantage of these incentives now will not only reduce their payback periods but will also be in a better competitive position for the long term.

CHAPTER 8

FINANCE

Even before the 2008 financial crisis, investors were awakening to the fact that financial success and good corporate citizenship go hand in hand. However, the implosion of the housing, equity, and debt markets exposed the need for increased regulation, transparency, and proper governance. Therefore, the debt, socially responsible investment, and venture capital sectors have all begun to pressure businesses to factor social, environmental, corporate governance, and climate issues into their financial statements, policies, disclosures, credit assessments, and lending guidelines. This is true long-term market changer and I believe this trend is only likely to increase with companies increasingly facing higher regulatory scrutiny and increased sustainability expectations by their lenders, customers and financiers.

Debt Markets

Lenders want the best return they can get at minimal risk. The mortgage and financial crises that hit the major investment firms, banks, and both Fannie Mae & Freddie Mac during the fall of 2008 only exasperated this as everyone now is scrambling to reduce risk to their assets.

For example, think about some of the companies we used to think of as big financial players:

Lehman Brothers	Merrill Lynch
Bear Stearns	Citibank
Wells Fargo	AIG

Morgan Stanley	JP Morgan Chase
IMB	Indymac Bank
Countrywide Financial	Bank of America
Wachovia	Washington Mutual

Of those, only four were still in business as of January 2009. In fact, it's no coincidence that four of the largest financial institutions that survived this crisis - Bank of America, Citibank, JP Morgan Chase, and Wells Fargo were all signatories to the Equator Principles – which considers social and environmental risks in project financing decisions.

Another guide for best practices for financial institutions for dealing with climate change is the "Climate Principles" launched in late 2008 by Credit Agricole, HSBC, Munich Re, Standard Chartered and Swiss Re. Some banks, for example, are now requiring prospective borrowers to meet certain GHG emission limits as part of their loan packages. Bank of America, J.P. Morgan Chase, Citigroup, Morgan Stanley, Credit Suisse, and Wells Fargo created "The Carbon Principle," a tool used to evaluate financial risk associated with financing electric power projects for their US power clients.[ci]

Additional frameworks such as the Equator Principles and the United Nations (UN) Principles for Responsible Investment are also being used by lenders to reshape their investment guidelines. In Europe, leading investment banks met to determine how best to incorporate climate into financial decisions, with the results becoming known as the London Accord.

The Equator Principles

Mentioned earlier, the Equator Principles are a comprehensive set of socially and environmentally responsible practices that over 63 of the world's major financial institutions have voluntarily adopted.[cii]

Borrowers that want loans from these signatories must categorize and fully disclose all risks associated with social and environmental performance and provide a mitigation plan for managing these risks. The Equator Principles also require consultation with and disclosure to affected communities, a mechanism for addressing grievances, and third-party verified review, monitoring and annual public reporting.[ciii] Though these types of requirements were unimaginable as recently as ten years ago, they are the future of debt markets.

The UN Principles for Responsible Investment

The UN Principles for Responsible Investment is another voluntary set of guidelines that provides investors with a range of options for not only fulfilling their fiduciary duty but also giving consideration to the Environmental, Social and corporate Governance (ESG) issues of the companies they choose. Whereas the Equator Principles are specifically for use by financial institutions, the UN Principles are intended to provide a framework for a broader section of the investment sector including asset owners, investment managers and professional service partners, managers, and professional service partners.

The UN Principles were developed by a multi-stakeholder group that represented 12 countries and was composed of investment industry experts, governmental organizations, and members from civil society and academia. The group's goal was to incorporate ESG issues into mainstream investment decision-making and ownership practices.

The six principles are listed below.[civ]

1. Incorporate ESG issues into investment analysis and decision-making processes.

2. Incorporate ESG issues into ownership policies and practices.

3. Seek appropriate disclosure on ESG issues by the entities invested.

4. Promote acceptance and implementation of the Principles within the investment industry.

5. Work together to enhance effectiveness in implementing the Principles.

6. Report on activities and progress toward implementing the Principles.

Currently, few companies are even aware of the rigorous requirements of these Principles; however, with renewed attention being paid to governance after 2008, business leaders should think about complying with them.

The London Accord[cv]

Representatives from a group of investment banks met in London in 2007 to determine how best to include climate change in financial decisions[cvi]. The meeting, which became known as The London Accord, determined that "a broad consensus has emerged that climate change presents a challenge - and that we *can* afford, economically, to solve it. The market got us into this mess - because the cost to the planet of our behavior was not properly priced. Now that we can see our way to pricing fully what the planet does for us, the market will get us out."[cvii] This Accord became a call to action for European financial institutions not already taking action.

What Major US Financial Institutions Are Doing

There is big money to be made through social and climate informed investment. Even though the largest lending institutions in the US are still struggling from the fallout of the toxic assets associated with the credit default swaps, many are taking bold action on climate change.

Citibank [cviii]

In 2007 Citibank did all of the following:

- Endorsed, along with more than 90 co-signers, the Joint Statement on Climate Change, at the Global Roundtable on Climate Change. Citi is also a signatory of the 3C (Combat Climate Change) Initiative.

- Created a standalone investment center called Sustainable Development Investments (SDI). The SDI program committed over $2 billion of private equity over the next ten years to renewable energy and clean technology, energy efficiency, carbon credit markets, waste, water management, and the sustainable forestry industry.

- Announced that it will direct an additional $50 billion over the next 10 years to address global climate change through investments, financings and related activities to support the commercialization and growth of renewable energy and clean technology.

- Committed $1 billion to the Clinton Climate Initiative to implement the new Energy Efficiency Building Retrofit Program in partnership with large city governments.

Bank of America

According to Anne Finucane, Global Marketing and Corporate Affairs Executive and Chair of Bank of America's Environmental Council, Bank of America recognizes that climate change and atmospheric pollution represent a risk to the ultimate stability and sustainability of their business. Therefore, the bank is committed to programs that set real and achievable targets for GHG reductions in both operations and investment.

Bank of America has done the following:

- Set a target to reduce their GHG emissions by 9% by 2009.

- Commissioned an independent study to evaluate the level of risk to the financing of intensive GHG emitting industries.

- Became the first financial services company to become a member of the EPA's Climate Leader Program, joined the CCX and the ECX, and sponsored the 2005 Institutional Investors Summit on Climate Risk.

HSBC

HSBC claims it is taking climate change even more seriously than its rivals, as it formed a groundbreaking, five-year partnership called The

HSBC Climate Partnership between itself and the Climate Group, Earthwatch Institute, Smithsonian Tropical Research Institute and World Wildlife Fund. HSBC's $100 million commitment to these four environmental charities aims to combat the urgent threat of climate change by inspiring action by individuals, businesses and governments worldwide.

To ensure that HSBC's approach to lending and investment reflects its business principles and values, sensitivity to society's expectations and an assessment of risk, the company:

- Adopted the Equator Principles and signed on to the UN Principles for Responsible Investment

- Published five sector guidelines and policies to complement its Environmental Risk Standard published in 2002 for its employees and customers.

- Is developing sustainability-focused business opportunities in the areas of low-carbon energy, water infrastructure, sustainable forestry and related agricultural commodities.

JP Morgan Chase

JP Morgan Chase has established numerous climate programs within both its investment bank and commercial bank to reduce GHG emissions internally and throughout its value chain. These include climate-mitigation policy that adds carbon disclosure and mitigation to its client review process.

Other products and research that JP Morgan Chase has implemented to address climate change are noted below:

- Carbon reduction products: JP Morgan Chase will work with clients to develop favorable financing solutions to fund development of relatively lower carbon-emitting technology solutions and investments in GHG reduction.

- Carbon reporting: JP Morgan Chase will annually report the aggregate GHG emissions from its power sector projects.

- Energy efficient mortgage: In mortgage loans products, the company will accommodate higher debt-to-income ratios for homes that are considered energy efficient.

- "Green" housing: JP Morgan Chase will continue to seek investments in low-income "green" housing that conserves energy and natural resources, promotes health, and provides easy access to jobs, schools, and services.

Equity Markets

Like debt markets, equity markets have also been incorporating issues related to climate change into their financial frameworks. This has primarily been done through instruments such as Socially Responsible Investing (SRI) and the Carbon Disclosure Project.

Before describing the intricacies of both SRI and the CDP, I think it's important to highlight some of the key factors that led to the mortgage and financial crisis of 2008. Certainly there were countless other activities that played a part but I want to highlight three big ones.

- The Gramm-Leach-Bliley Act: 1999

  This was signed into law by President Clinton and repealed provisions of the Glass-Steagall Act that prohibited banks from owning other financial companies such as investment banks.

- The Commodity Futures Modernization Act: 2000

  This allowed the trade of credit-default swaps.

- The SEC suspension of the Net Capital Rule

  The government imposed limits on debt that investment banks such as Goldman Sachs, Merrill Lynch, Lehman Brothers, Bear Stearns, and Morgan Stanley could assume was removed.

We all remember what happened and are still feeling the effects, but I think it's important to highlight some of the major casualties, to help put the importance of SRI in better context.

1) Foreclosures hit roughly 2.26 million in 2008 with the foreclosure rate estimated to increase another 4.25% by the end of 2009 according to Meredith Whitney, an Oppenheimer & Company Analyst.[cix]

2) The markets tanked. We highlighted the fate of many major US financial institutions, but neglected to discuss the larger market impacts. The Dow started 2008 at 13,043. By November 20th it collapsed to below 7,600 for the first time in 5 years. This represented an astonishing drop of more than 34% in two months.

3) Internationally, many stock exchanges followed our lead:

   • Japan's Nikkei 225 hit a 26 year low.

   • Iceland's stock exchanged crashed 81% during the month of October.

   • Argentina's Merval and Brazil's Bovespa indices had their biggest one-month percentage losses since their economies' crises of 1998, with the Merval falling 37% and the Bovespa losing 25%.

All of this all occurred even after the Federal Reserve and Congress offered a $700 billion rescue package in October, the EU's $2.3 Trillion rescue package, and the first ever coordinated interest rate cut by the following federal treasuries:

• US Federal Reserve	• Britain
• China	• Canada
• European Central Bank	• Sweden
	• Switzerland

Additional stimuli have already been proposed for early 2009 and others are likely later in the year and in 2010. Could any of this have been prevented? Many economists believe that if there had been greater emphasis in following the guidelines of SRI and the CDP, that at least some of this crisis could have been averted.

Socially Responsible Investing

Socially Responsible Investing (SRI) refers to the incorporation of the investor's social or ethical criteria in the investment decision-making process.

Before I write about the specifics of SRI, I want to point out that "a full dozen years before some Wall Street experts and regulators reluctantly started to accept the possibility of an impending subprime mortgage debacle in the US, SRI and faith-based organizations started urging that major corrective action be taken to reduce subprime lending risks to homeowners, communities and investors at large." [cx]

Surprisingly some within the faith community were sounding the loudest alarm bells. According to Laura Berry, executive director, Interfaith Center on Corporate Responsibility, "Time and time again, the prophetic voice of faith has allowed our members to anticipate emerging areas of corporate responsibility. ...before anyone else, members expressed concerns related to predatory lending practices, inappropriate underwriting standards and the potential consequences of securitization of debt instruments."[cxi]

SRI has grown dramatically over the past decade due to a number of factors including:

- increasing customer awareness.

- investor preference for matching financial investments with ethical and moral values.

- the comparable financial performance SRI has been able to demonstrate against other traditional funds.

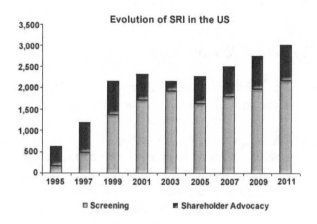

Figure 26. Evolution of SRI in the US.

Source: Social Investment Forum Foundation, Celent[cxii]

Beyond these facts, SRI is a booming market globally. As of 2008 it had a worth of about $2.71 trillion dollars in the US alone, and nearly one out of every ten dollars under professional management in the United States belonged to socially responsible investment funds like Calvert, Trillium, and Portfolio 21.[cxiiicxiv] Celent, a financial consultancy, predicts that the SRI market in the US will grow beyond $3 trillion within the next few years.[cxv] These trends are not just confined to the US; as the European SRI market grew by $892 billion in the last two years.

How SRI Is Done

There are three main ways SRI investing is done:

- Investment screening

- Shareholder advocacy & resolutions

- Community investing

Investment Screening

The practice of SRI used to focus more on "negative screens" that weeded out the types of companies that investors did not want to support; these screens are still commonly used, especially in the assessment of industries such as:

tobacco	weapons manufacturing
alcohol	arms dealing
gambling	nuclear energy
natural resource extraction	

In addition to industry filters, some SRI negative screens eliminate businesses that operate in regions ruled by violent or corrupt government regimes, such as Sudan or Burma.

A more recent trend has focused on trying to effect positive change and reward good behavior, or at least good intentions, by supporting companies that are actively pursuing the improvement of their social and environmental impacts. This is still a very small component of SRI screening but has gained momentum in recent years.

As the largest US public pension fund, the California Public Employees' Retirement System (CalPERS) has been a leader in this regard, and positioned itself to capitalize from climate-friendly investments and is innovating beyond traditional negative and positive screens in its investment strategies. Some examples of CalPERS' unique investment activities are listed below:

- $185 million invested in clean technology [cxvi]

- Working with key players in the transportation utilities and oil and gas sectors to more fully disclose their environmental data [cxvii]

- Leveraging investments in real estate to support green building, with a goal of reducing energy consumption in its real estate portfolio by 20 percent over the next five years [cxviii]

- Directing $2.4 billion (1% of total assets) into sustainable forestry to profit from the emerging forest carbon credits market [cxix]

Shareholder Advocacy

Another form of SRI is shareholder advocacy, which most commonly involves shareholders filing a resolution calling for a specific action from the company. Typical resolutions involve human rights, working conditions, and executive compensation; increasingly though, shareholder resolutions on climate issues are gaining momentum. In 2007, 43 climate-related shareholder resolutions were filed with US companies, leading to positive actions by businesses such as ConocoPhillips, Wells Fargo, and Hartford Insurance.[cxx]

Additionally, a group of institutional investors controlling nearly \$4 trillion in assets signed a statement urging Congress to pass strict laws to curb GHG emissions.[cxxi] These SRI functions are still in use today and for companies seeking additional equity investment, they need to be aware of the media and brand risk that may be brought through shareholder resolutions.

Community Investing

Community investing was the original type of SRI, usually practiced by local banks; however it has now evolved to channel affordable credit to communities underserved by traditional credit markets. These investors often accept slightly below-market rates of financial return to encourage investment that can create jobs, build homes, finance community facilities, and rebuild neighborhoods, all of which positively affect the economic development of a community in the long run.

Although not formally an SRI process, a new type of community investment has emerged known as responsible property investment (RPI). RPI is a framework to help investors consider environmental and social aspects when making real estate investment decisions. At its core, RPI is an investment strategy that helps investors identify risks and opportunities and create value. Because climate change and energy pose significant risks and opportunities, such considerations are central to RPI.

Improved Market Performance

One of the major arguments commonly voiced against socially responsible investing is the misperception that SRI funds provide a lower return on investment than do traditional investments. Now that SRI has been around for a while, however, there is enough data to definitively show that SRI funds have an equivalent performance to traditional funds over both the short-and long-term. In fact many have beaten the Standard and Poor's 500 (S&P 500) on a consistent basis over the past 10 years.*cxxii*

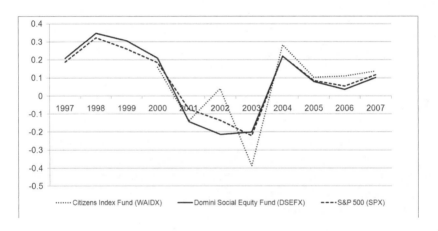

Figure 27. SRI performance against the S&P 500 1997-2007.

Figure 27 above demonstrates how the Citizens Index Fund and the Domini Social Equity Fund performed from 1997-2007 against the S&P 500. As you can see, SRI funds flourished in the 1990s during the dot.com boom and recovered robustly after the market collapse of 2001 and 2002. This is especially important because the recent foreclosure crisis in the housing market has many economists worried about a possible recession, which is just the type of market condition that would give traditional investors pause about SRI. The exact opposite should occur because SRI may be a smart hedge against a prolonged market downturn.

According to Bruce Herbert, CEO of Newground Social Investment, "SRI analysts have a broader and more thoroughgoing screening process than non-SRI investors (who typically only examine the numbers over-and-over); therefore companies with potential problems are frequently excluded from SRI portfolios. For example, many SRI investors had avoided being in Enron, Tyco, and WorldCom when the 2001-2002 accounting scandals hit. Companies that looked good one day from a numbers-only perspective suffered terribly the next, due to social and governance factors that Wall Street had by-and-large neglected."

Moreover, you can see above that when the markets rallied in 2003 and 2004 and the S & P 500 increased by 22% in 2004, SRI funds matched or exceeded this rally:

- Citizens Index Fund increased by 28.19%.

- Domini Social Equity Fund increased by 21.85%.

- Calvert Large Cap Growth Fund increased by 17.49%.[cxxiii]

Sustainability Indices & Reports

Complementing the growth of SRI funds has been the emergence of various sustainability indices. The goal of these indices is to track and demonstrate the financial performance of those companies with proactive environmental and social performance.

The major indices are:

- The Dow Jones Sustainability Indices

- The Financial Times Stock Exchange for Good

- The Michael Jantzi Social Index

Dow Jones Sustainability Indices (DJSI World)

The most popular and the first global index tracking the financial performance of the leading sustainability-driven companies worldwide was the Dow Jones Sustainability Index. Its goal is to provide asset managers with reliable and objective benchmarks to manage sustainability portfolios. Currently the DJSI World examines the top 10% of the biggest 2,500 companies in the Dow Jones World Index in terms of economic, environmental and social criteria.[cxxiv]

Financial Times Stock Exchange for Good (FTSE4Good) Index

The FTSE4Good Index is designed to measure the performance of companies that meet globally recognized corporate responsibility standards and to facilitate investment in those companies. Launched in 2001, the FTSE4Good recently introduced climate change criteria, and since January 2007, companies designated as "high impact" within the index have had to meet stronger criteria to maintain their places within the index.

Michael Jantzi Social Index (MJSI)

Jantzi Research launched the Jantzi Social Index on January 1, 2000 as an index of common stock index including 60 Canadian companies that pass a set of broadly-based social and environmental screens. From its inception through January 31, 2008, the JSI achieved an annualized return of 7.69%, while the S&P/TSX Composite and the S&P/TSX 60 had annualized returns of 7.68% and 7.55% respectively, over the same period.[cxxv] The MJSI is one of the more rigorous and credible indices in the world and has at times outperformed the FTSE4GOOD and DJSI indices.

The Carbon Disclosure Project

In addition to SRI funds, efforts like the Carbon Disclosure Project (CDP) have emerged to report companies' climate policies and actions. The CDP is an independent not-for-profit organization that strives to create a lasting relationship between shareholders and corporations regarding the implications of climate change on their business operations. CDP signatories are a coalition of asset managers and owners that are sending a clear signal to the world's largest publicly traded companies, requesting planning, action, and corporate transparency on the risks and opportunities posed on their organization by climate change.[cxxvi]

The CDP is not another fly by night environmental non-profit; it operates out of New York City and London and has partners in 16 of the world's major economies to help deliver the program globally. The CDP works with 3,000 of the largest corporations in the world to disclose their carbon reduction strategies to investors. According to its website the CDP has:

- Established the world's largest repository of GHG emissions and energy use data accounting for some 26% of human-caused CO_2 emissions.

- Started to establish a globally used standard for emissions and energy reporting.

- Examined the 265 major electric utilities globally (high GHG emitters).

- Obtained backing from blue chip investors including HSBC, JP Morgan Chase, Bank of America, Goldman Sachs, American International Group, and State Street Corp.

- The CDP and its 385+ members recognize the potential market impacts of such actions. As of 2008, this group represented an unprecedented $57 trillion in assets under management—up from $31 trillion in 2006.

Equity Screens

GS Sustain[cxxvii]

Goldman Sachs, the most respected investment fund on Wall Street has also gotten into the game. It recently launched a new product called GS Sustain which uses a proprietary environmental, social and corporate governance (ESG) framework compared against the economy, their industry, society, and the environment.

GS Sustain incorporates the ten principles of the UN Global Impact covering human rights, labor standards, environment, and anticorruption.

Goldman is doing this because it believes eco-efficiency and leadership in environmental performance are a proxy for management quality over the long term. Goldman Sachs plans to use its ESG framework to provide a consistent approach for analyzing objective, quantitative measures around governing environmental and social performance. For example, one way Goldman is doing this is by assessing a company's energy consumption relative to its asset base as a metric to measure cost control and efficiency of resource use.

SRI has proven its financial competitiveness and established a strong performance historically, even during market downturns or recession. With the positive correlation between sustainability performance and management quality, investors no longer have to feel like they are making a tradeoff when they choose SRI.

Venture Capital

Venture capital is another type of equity investment that is seeing major growth trends related to sustainability. Clean technology, which incorporates both renewable and energy efficiency(both key to fighting climate change) fared as well or better than other VC sectors during the financial crisis of 2008 and is promising to be the next big thing in the venture capital arena. *cxxviii* In fact, clean technology has moved up to become the third-largest North American venture capital investment category, with almost $1.6 billion, or 6% of all venture investments, behind software and biotechnology.[cxxix]

In 2007, investments in clean technology grew to over $2.6 billion invested from a scant $663 million as recently as 2004.[cxxx, cxxxi]

Year	Total Venture Investments (US$ Billions)	Energy Technology Investments (US$ Millions)	Energy Technology Percentage of Venture Total
2000	$105.1	$599	0.6%
2001	$40.6	$584	1.4%
2002	$22	$483	2.2%
2003	$19.7	$446	2.3%
2004	$22.5	$663	2.9%
2005	$23	$1,038	4.5%
2006	$26.5	$1,555	5.9%
2007	$29.4	$2,665	9.1%

Source: New Energy Finance with supporting data from Nth Power and Clean Edge. NOTE: New Energy Finance's energy-tech VC numbers include investment in renewable energy, biofuels, low-carbon technologies, and the carbon markets. VC figures are for development and initial commercialization of technologies, products and services, and do not include private investments in public equity (PIPE) or expansion capital deals.

Figure 28. Venture capital investments in clean technology.[cxxxii]

Investments in Clean Technology

The main reasons behind heightened investment in clean technology are increased market demand, realization that solutions to climate are necessary, the existence of a lucrative market, and high growth potential.

As prices of traditional energy sources continue to rise, the global market for clean energy sources such as biofuels, solar and wind energy, are expected to more than quadruple to $167 billion by 2015.[cxxxiii] Meanwhile, the world energy market is worth an estimated $5 trillion. As pressure mounts to develop renewable energy, clean technology may "create an initial public offering (IPO) frenzy that could blow the internet boom out of the water."[cxxxiv] There is huge money to be made from clean technology products and services; otherwise, venture capitalists would not be paying attention.

Following John Doerr's Lead

Many investors, angels and venture capitalists, take their cue from famous Silicon Valley venture capitalist John Doerr of Kleiner Perkins (KPCB), who made his name and fortune with early investments in Netscape Communications, Amazon.com, and Google, among others. Prior to Doerr's commitment there was uncertainty among the venture capital community as to whether clean technology was a viable long-term investment sector and not just the next dot.com bust.

Doerr and his firm are placing big bets on the emerging clean technology sector which he has stated could become as lucrative as information technology and biotechnology. KPCB expects to fully dedicate up to one-third of all new funding to clean technologies that help provide cleaner energy, transportation, air, and water by 2009.

Climate change is shaping up be the defining challenge of our generation and the stakes are high. Doerr has been quoted as saying that "it's probably the largest economic opportunity of the 21st century."[cxxxv]

The following chart provides a brief comparison between the internet boom and the anticipated green tech boom.

	INTERNET	GREEN TECH
MADE OF:	Bits, pixels	Atoms, molecules
WHAT IS AT STAKE:	Finding friends on FaceBook	Life on the planet
CAPITAL NEEDED:	LOW: Google needed $25 million	HIGH: Hundreds of millions
TIME TO SUCCESS:	QUICK: 3 to 5 years	LONGER: 5 to 10 years
MARKET POTENTIAL:	LARGE: Billions	ENORMOUS: Trillions

Differences between the IT and Green Tech booms

Conclusion

Former Vice President and Nobel Prize Recipient Al Gore compared the financial risks facing investors in carbon-intensive industries with the meltdown in the market for subprime mortgages: "The assumption that you can safely invest in assets that come from business models that assume carbon is free is an assumption that is about to go splat. Many companies have lots of assets in your portfolios that are chock full of 'subprime' carbon assets."[cxxxvi] This is something to take very seriously, especially considering what the subprime mortgage crisis did towards creating our current economic situation.

The financial industry, with its considerable leverage, is stepping in to fight climate change through increasingly stringent social and environmental standards. As companies look to expand or move to take advantage of opportunities in emerging markets, investors and lenders are not going to sit on the sidelines, they are and will increasingly require companies to detail the social, environmental, and climate implications of their actions to obtain financing.

Companies need to also be aware of both the huge financial opportunities and risks that climate change presents to their business model.

CHAPTER 9

INSURANCE

The number of extreme weather events has increased over the past 40 years, which has dramatically increased insurance risk and financial losses. The insurance industry, a major force in influencing corporate behavior, is not going to stand by and absorb financial and property losses due to these events, especially in a down economy. Business leaders need to take note because the insurance industry is moving to reduce its risk and potential liability by developing new policies and products around climate change in the same way other insurance policies protect against fire, flood, tornado, or even hurricane damage. This chapter is therefore focused on providing an overview of how climate change will impact the insurance industry, what insurers are doing on this issue, and what this means for business.

Industry Overview

Insurance companies are exposed to climate change as both fiduciaries and investment vehicles. The sectors' income statements and balance sheets are affected in interdependent ways, but

> "The insurance industry holds considerable power and potential to encourage positive change on the issue of global warming." — Michelle Rupp, NRG Seattle[j]

both have great risk exposure to an increase in extreme weather-related events. Thus, the incentive to reduce their potential liability from climate change is considerable.

The reinsurance industry, which serves as the backbone of the industry by insuring insurance companies, has been paying attention to the risks of climate change for years. Major reinsurance firms such as Swiss Re identified climate change as an emerging risk as early as 20 years ago, and it has since evolved into an important component of the company's long-term risk-management strategy. Swiss Re believes that tackling this issue is in the interest of shareholders, customers, employees, the wider stakeholder community, and society in general.

Swiss Re, Munich Re, and many of the other major reinsurance companies are now ardently pursuing objectives such as:

- Finding ways to measure and integrate climate change risks into risk-management and underwriting frameworks.

- Assessing the climate change risk of their current and potential clients.

- Creating new products and services to mitigate climate risk.

- Raising awareness about climate change risks through risk dialogue with clients, employees, and the public.

- Measuring their own carbon footprints and ensuring transparent, annual emissions reporting.[cxxxvii]

Additionally, an increasing number of companies and investors are realizing that climate change carries significant economic implications for shareholder value. The particular relevance for insurers is due to the close correlation between underwriting losses due to extreme weather events and the corresponding effects on the value of capital market investments. To this end, many insurers are now looking at advanced risk models that consider multiple catastrophic events, along with environmental factors such as increased temperatures, warmer waters, and changes in accident frequency and severity patterns.

Businesses should expect increasing pressure from their insurers to calculate and disclose climate risk, develop mitigation plans, and prepare for new and more stringent policy requirements that may mean increases in reporting, higher premiums, or more difficulty in obtaining insurance. In fact, there have already been numerous cases in the US in which this has occurred and companies have had to address climate policies during the renewal of their Executives and Officers (E&O) liability insurance.

Risk to Insurance Companies

There has been a dramatic increase in the number of natural disasters in the US over the past 10 years. Although we cannot say flatly that climate change caused particular natural disasters, we *can* say that climate change is causing extreme weather events to occur more frequently and with greater intensity, thus increasing risk, liability, and financial losses. In particular, 2005 saw how the major loss events of Hurricanes Katrina and Rita strained the resources of insurance companies and subsequently affected profitability and insurance companies' ability to fulfill their responsibilities.

After the tragedy of Hurricane Katrina, estimates of damage and economic losses ranged from $14 billion to $225 billion in insured damages. Using computer models, experts have estimated that the insurance industry will pay out from $15 billion to $60 billion.[cxxxviii] Hurricane Rita's estimated cost of damages was approximately $6 billion.[cxxxix]

Weather-related events were the primary cause of insurance losses between 1987 and 2005, amounting to over $320 billion, according to the Government Accountability Office.[cxl] In fact, according to the Insurance Information Institute, consumers have seen homeowner insurance costs along the East and Gulf coasts rise from 20% to 100% since 2004 because of this.[cxli]

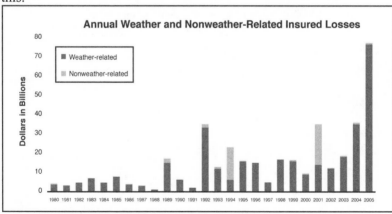

Source: GAO analysis of PCS, NFIP, and FCIC data

Private Insurers paid $243.5 billion – over 75 percent of the total weather-related losses reviewed. The two major federal insurance programs – NFIP and FCIC – paid the remaining $77.7 billion of the $321.2 billion in weather-related loss payments reviewed. NFIP paid about $34.1 billion or about 11 percent of the total weather-related loss payments reviewed during this period. As illustrated in Figure 2, claims averaged about $1.3 billion per year, but ranged from $75.7 million in 1988 to $16.7 billion in 2005.

Figure 29. Weather-related insurance losses are increasing.[cxlii]

AIR Worldwide, a leading catastrophe modeling firm, reported that insured losses are expected to double roughly every 10 years because of increases in construction costs, number of structures, and differences in characteristics.*cxliii* These costs will be passed down to businesses, and consumers must plan for higher costs in the future.

Given all of these changes and risks, it is in the best interest of businesses to draw attention to these issues and develop mitigation plans for their infrastructure, supply chains, projects, and day-to-day operations. In fact, as climate legislation takes hold and a cap-and-trade market emerges to put a cost on emitting greenhouse gas, it may be difficult for some industries to be insured at all without stringent and detailed climate-change policies.

Although there are many risks, with risk comes opportunity. A summary of opportunities for the insurance industry is provided in Figure 30.

Opportunities of Climate Change		
	Risks	**Opportunities**
Property & Casualty	Property damage from weather events and increased risk to business lines	Increased demand for traditional and new risk transfer solutions such as catastrophe bonds and weather derivatives
	Demographic changes, population displacements that create social, political, and economic instability	Potential increase in governmental sponsored solutions. ie. For flood risks and crop losses.
Asset Management	Hidden GHG liabilities impair market values of securities, increased energy costs, and real estate impaired by weather events	Improved investment analysis due to disclosure of potential carbon assets and liabilities
Operational Risk	Reputational damage due to inadequate response to climate change issues	Long term reputational stability and competitive advantage through successful carbon strategy

Figure 30. Climate change poses risks & opportunities for the insurance industry.*cxliv*

Industry Association Involvement

The issue of climate change has been addressed for many years by reinsurers and European insurance companies, but the rest of the world is catching up quickly, especially the US. This is not an issue that just a few progressive or green insurers are paying attention to, either. Entire industry associations are getting involved:

- The National Association of Insurance Commissioners created a Climate Change and Global Warming Task Force.[cxlv]

- In an effort to mitigate risks, the US insurance industry formed a coalition called ProtectingAmerica.org to better protect local communities and the economy from extreme weather events.

- Climatenandinsurance.org was created by the National Association of Mutual Insurance Companies to provide a place for industry professionals to understand climate change and its impact on the insurance industry.[cxlvi]

- The Institute for Business and Home Safety has created a website to help insurers and their clients reduce the social and economic effects of natural disasters and property losses.[cxlvii]

Examples of What Insurers Are Doing

As mentioned above, many insurers are already taking an outward position regarding climate change and are realigning business practices to incorporate this issue into their operations. Companies seeking renewals of policies or to limit their premium increases need to be aware of these trends in the insurance industry. Proactive companies can prepare now for demands from their insurers by analyzing their carbon footprint and developing climate change strategies.

Some of the larger insurers have been quite forthcoming as to their stance and have developed action plans to help form a solution. A few of the larger insurers have come out with public positions around this issue. Major initiatives include innovative product development and incorporation of climate issues into existing insurance policy offerings. Some specific actions being taken by industry leaders are covered below.

AIG (even before being bailed out by the Federal Reserve)

AIG created corporate policy that supports development of strategic products, services, and policies designed to help customers mitigate climate risk.

The insurance giant also designed new products that support the carbon market and insures against projects that fail to generate tradable carbon-emission reductions. For example, AIG Environmental® works with customers to better manage environmental risks and to remediate environmental damages.

AIG adopted a public statement that climate change poses a threat to human health, well being, ecosystems, and to its customers. AIG also became the first insurance company to join (in 2007) the United States Climate Action Partnership (USCAP), an alliance of major businesses and leading climate and environmental groups that came together to call on the federal government to enact legislation on GHG reduction.

Allstate Insurance[cxlviii]

Allstate revised some of its homeowner insurance policies and decided not to renew others in areas of especially high weather-related risk.

The company also requires borrowers to comply with new environmental policies and expects borrowers to engage in sound environmental management practices. This includes issues relating to flood plains, wetlands, radon, asbestos, lead-based paint, and indoor air quality and mold control.

State Farm[cxlix]

State Farm is investing in tools and techniques to model severe weather conditions to price and underwrite insurance for their clients.

In the case of Hurricane Katrina, State Farm's brand value was tarnished and received very negative PR because of disputes between

Katrina victims about what was covered by the insurance company and what was not. State Farm was portrayed by the media in a very negative manner with accusations of "altering the findings in its Katrina report so that State Farm would not have to pay."[cl] Customer lawsuits and complaints were lodged against State Farm for not covering water damage due to the hurricane, including from Mississippi Senator Trent Lott and the state's attorney general, Jim Hood, who sued five large insurers due to their response to this natural disaster.[cli]

Esurance

Esurance is the only insurance company to have built its business model around an environmental message.[clii]

"Must Reads" on Climate and Insurance

Ceres, a national network of investment funds, has published two in-depth reports that examine the impact of climate change on the insurance industry, and business leaders should be familiar with both of these to get a true idea of what to expect in the future:

- "Availability and Affordability of Insurance under Climate Change: A Growing Challenge for the U.S." This 2005 report provides a warning to companies to expect changes in insurance availability, affordability, and coverage depending on companies' mitigation policies and actions on climate.[cliii]

- "From Risk to Opportunity: How Insurers Can Proactively and Profitably Manage Climate Change." This 2006 publication is another "must read" for business leaders that are wondering how to reduce their risk and premiums by making climate mitigation part of their company practices. It provides an overview of what insurers are doing to adapt to the changing market risks and opportunities related to climate change.[cliv]

Conclusion

The insurance industry understands better than most the potential financial, social, and environmental risks that climate change presents. Businesses need to understand that their insurance companies are not going to wait to mitigate their own climate risks. Changes are coming to insurance policies that relate to climate and will affect their clients' policies. In order to keep your business insurance premiums down, you will have to develop and constantly update your climate mitigation plans.

CHAPTER 10

SUPPLY CHAIN MANAGEMENT

Companies are becoming increasingly aware of the need to address sustainability within their supply chain. Businesses have always relied on their supply chains to deliver value to their customers, but as I will demonstrate in this chapter, leading businesses are recognizing the potential for supply chains to contribute to the value of their brands, sustainability performance, and bottom line, even during times of economic uncertainty.

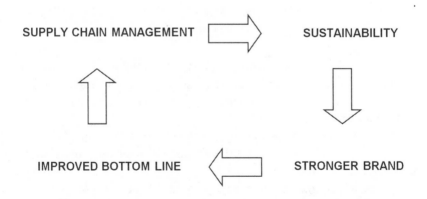

Figure 31. The reinforcing loop of sustainable supply chain management.[clv]

None of this is truly revolutionary or groundbreaking because successful companies have long known that the more efficient their supply chain, the more cost effective it is. Proper supply chain management also presents an opportunity to reduce GHG emissions and waste, strengthen an organization's position in the marketplace, and demonstrate responsibility to customers.

Opportunities to improve climate performance exist at every juncture of the supply chain and may be the best way for companies to make an impact, especially companies not traditionally perceived as being "green." Leaders such as Hewlett Packard (HP), Wal-Mart, Starbucks, Nike, and S.C. Johnson have taken climate change very seriously by leveraging their weight throughout the supply network and are reaping huge rewards through innovative, cost saving, climate-friendly solutions.

> "Taking waste and non-renewable energy out of our supply chain reduces the amount of pollution and greenhouse gases our suppliers send into the atmosphere." —Lee Scott, CEO, Wal-Mart[k]

Businesses face the challenge of providing products and services that are sustainable through all stages of the supply chain or risk losing market share to those who manage to do so. Therefore, throughout this chapter, I've outlined not only the opportunities for improved financial and climate performance but also specific examples of what companies can do to improve their supply chains.

What Is a Sustainable Supply Chain?

Supply chains consist of suppliers, vendors, manufacturers, distributors, retailers, and consumers. Businesses have different opportunities to affect change depending on what role along the supply chain a company occupies.

Therefore, suppliers are increasingly being asked to disclose social, environmental, and climate-related information about the materials they are supplying and about their business policies and practices. Purchasers are starting to use this information to give preference to more sustainable suppliers. Being proactive in this market space can help businesses create competitive advantage and access new market opportunities while also benefiting from cost savings.

Numerous companies are now making sustainability and climate performance part of their vendor requirements, including Wal-Mart which has been asking sustainability related questions of its 60,000 suppliers. These questions have led to tangible actions such as partnering with Unilever to repackage its laundry detergent to make it three times more concentrated. I mentioned Unilever earlier when talking about its shampoo; below are some annual benefits of concentrating its detergent, including:

- Saving more than 400 million gallons of water.

- Saving more than 95 million pounds of plastic resin.

- Saving more than 125 million pounds of cardboard.

- Freeing up valuable shelf space.

- Reducing shipping and storage costs (and resultant GHG emissions).

- Educating consumers and showing them an environmental benefit without having to change their behavior.

Additionally, when the rest of the laundry detergent industry implements the same changes, the impact will be four times greater.[clvi]

LEAN

LEAN is the leading framework for making business processes more efficient and streamlined to eliminate waste and any activities that don't add value. Although LEAN is not specifically a sustainability or climate-change strategy, it inherently contributes to these goals because of its focus on efficiency. Eliminating waste and streamlining processes makes supply chains more sustainable, cost-effective, and reduces climate impacts at the same time.

The Changing Relationships between Businesses and their Supply Chains

Trends in Sustainable Supply Chain Management

Three of the major trends shaping the world of supply chain management are

- More direct and engaging relationships between companies and their suppliers.

- Greater information exchange and transparency up and down the supply chain.

- CSR guidelines asking companies about supply chain management.

These trends are arising in the larger context of an ever-changing business landscape that now includes climate response.[clvii]

Many companies are taking strong stands on sustainable supply chain processes and are working to influence their supply chain partners. As mentioned earlier, Wal-Mart is one of the most aggressive in managing their supply chain relationships, first to encourage cost-cutting measures and now to further its financial goals by promoting sustainability.

> "Companies are expected to ensure that products and services are both more sustainable in their usage and disposal, and are produced, packaged, and shipped using more socially and environmentally responsible manufacturing practices." —Business for Social Responsibility[l]

In 2008, Wal-Mart began using a sustainability scorecard to rate 60,000 suppliers. The initiative has potential to save 667,000 metric tons of CO_2, the equivalent of removing 213,000 trucks annually from the road.[clviii] Customers will be able to use the scorecard as a tool when making purchasing decisions.

Many large companies besides Wal-Mart are beginning to measure suppliers' environmental and climate impacts, including HP, L'Oreal, PepsiCo, and Reckitt Benckiser, which have joined the Carbon Disclosure Project's Supply Chain Leadership Collaboration. Companies that are part of the collaboration encourage their top 50 suppliers to report GHG emissions data, emissions-reduction targets, and climate-change strategy.[clix] This is something for all businesses to pay attention to, big or small, because as these firms attempt to lower their carbon footprints, they will start making stricter demands throughout their supply chains. The trend is moving in this direction, providing great opportunities for small, innovative businesses to gain a competitive advantage through sustainability supply-chain leadership.

The old relationships of the past, which were characterized by rigid boundaries and often focused solely on price and performance, have begun to evolve over the past decade. From the three trends stated earlier in this chapter, two methodologies for affecting change within the supply chain have emerged: supplier assessment and supplier engagement.

Supplier Assessment

HP typifies the assessment strategy through its distribution of a code of conduct to all members of its supply chain and periodic audits to confirm compliance. Supplier assessment initiatives can be very useful for companies with large or complex global supply chains as they can determine a new supplier's sustainability status even before accepting it into the supply chain. Certain industries such as electronics and apparel have already shown a tendency to favor assessment strategies.

Supplier Engagement

Engagement strategies are generally favored by small- to medium-sized companies that can better implement sustainability in their supply chains through a combination of employee engagement, trainings, and sharing of best practices. This education then enables a supplier to set its own climate goals and work towards them in a long-term partnership that is both financially successful and sustainable.

Both assessment and engagement strategies facilitate the collection, management, and exchange of large amounts of information. Although this requires significant infrastructure, it leads to greater transparency and more efficient and sustainable supply chain systems, which benefits both the environment *and* the bottom line.

Upstream Supply Chain Climate Solutions

Addressing sustainability in the supply chain has the advantage of being an "upstream" solution and packs a huge punch by influencing many companies.

Dole recently announced a major climate-and-supply-chain effort in its Costa Rica production, committing to becoming climate neutral by 2012. As part of this pledge, Dole is:

- Increasing rail transport to reduce GHG emissions from its truck fleet.

- Reducing fossil fuel–based agricultural inputs to reduce its dependence on oil.

- Updating its refrigerated container fleet to be more efficient.[clx]

In many sectors, companies that have looked at their supply chains through the sustainability lens have found significant opportunities to save money both in the short and long term. Certain aspects of the supply chain have greater impact opportunities than others, depending on the sector and business being considered. The following pages discuss companies that have realized financial or brand benefits by taking action at strategic points in their supply chains.

Raw Materials

Whether producing widgets or selling goods, companies can make procurement decisions that are good for business and address climate change. Below are some specific strategies that apply to both.

Reduced Use of Petroleum-Based Substances

The surfboard company Homeblown found that switching from conventional petroleum-based materials to biodegradable alternatives was cost competitive and better for the environment. Homeblown now sources 50% of its ingredients from plant resins for its Biofoam surfboards without sacrificing profits.[clxi]

A number of retailers have also begun to phase out the petroleum-based poly vinyl chloride (PVC) from packaging and merchandise. Sears recently joined Wal-Mart and Target in making this pledge.[clxii] By reducing the use of hazardous materials in their products, companies often realize financial benefits from reduced training, handling, workers' compensation, and disposal costs.[clxiii]

Sustainable Wood

Home improvement giant Home Depot has helped more vendors transition to wood certified by the Forest Stewardship Council (FSC) than any other retailer in the US. It has done this largely through a preferential treatment program that launched in 1999. As a result, the company is the largest supplier of certified wood on the planet.[clxiv] These efforts help fight climate change through responsible land use, which allows forests to serve as carbon sinks, while also providing brand value to the company as customers feel good about buying wood from Home Depot.

Storage/Inventory

Streamlining inventory, reducing storage square footage, and using just-in-time inventory principles can lower operating and carrying costs while also lowering climate impacts like energy use and waste. Public

Service Electric and Gas Company (PSEG) used a number of these measures to address inventory inefficiencies and realized savings of more than \$2 million since inception, while decreasing waste.[clxv]

Packaging

Making changes in packaging can provide substantial payoffs for suppliers and customers alike. There are three ways to reduce your carbon footprint through packaging: (1) reduce it, (2) reuse and recycle it, and (3) redesign it to be biodegradable.

Using less packaging is the most cost effective strategy, but different packaging choices can allow companies to reap multiple benefits, as I mention below.

Reduced Packaging

Almost a decade ago, Nike redesigned their shoe boxes, shifting from eighteen styles to two and eliminated 8,000 tons of raw material fiber use per year.[clxvi] The new boxes are 10 percent lighter, benefiting retailers through lower transportation and storage costs, and are made of 100% post-consumer recycled material while providing the same performance as the old boxes.[clxvii]

The North Face removed hang tags and tissue paper from footwear packaging. This not only saved them money but also eliminates thousands of tons of waste that had no brand value to the end consumer.

Reusable Packaging

Many companies have switched from using traditional boxes and wooden pallets to reusable recycled plastic containers and pallets. General Motors has saved \$12 million in disposal costs through its use of reusable shipping containers while also decreasing damage to products and workers' compensation costs.[clxviii]

Biodegradable Materials

This is another alternative that is starting to find more traction. Analysts project that "the biodegradable packaging market could grow by as much as 20 percent per year,"[clxix] especially as customers are increasingly uncomfortable with all the waste associated with disposable plastics and Styrofoam. Amidst this, a number of smaller companies have emerged to develop biodegradable and compostable packaging materials, and larger companies like DuPont and Cargill have announced partnerships to develop biodegradable starch and plant-based polymers that could replace plastic in packaging.[clxx] In the environmentally conscious Pacific Northwest, Tully's coffee decided to move to a compostable cup as a market differentiator from its larger competitors, Starbucks and Peet's.

Transportation/Distribution

Fuel prices are soaring, forcing companies to be more strategic and efficient in the transportation of their products and goods as a financial business necessity. Loading trucks more efficiently, using more efficient routing and logistical information, driving more–fuel-efficient vehicles, and minimizing idling all reduce costs for companies and have positive financial and climate benefit.

Load Trucks as Full as Possible

Packing trucks efficiently is an easy way to reduce the number of trips and vehicle miles. For example, Dell has rearranged how it packs and deliver products and has gone from an average truckload weight of 18,000 pounds to 22,000 pounds, resulting in fewer trips overall, even if each trip burns more fuel.[clxxi]

3M[clxxii]

By packing pallets on two levels, 3M eliminated the use of truck cabs with sleeping berths because all trips could be made in one day.

FINANCIAL	BRAND	SUSTAINABILITY
Saved $110,000 per year.	This complimented several other environmental initiatives the company had undertaken.	Reduced truckloads by 40 percent. Cabs without births are lighter, use less gas, and therefore produce fewer GHG emissions.

S.C. Johnson[clxxiii]

S.C. Johnson initiated a truckload-utilization project that aimed to balance maximum capacity with maximum weight in loading to reduce total number of truck loads.

FINANCIAL	BRAND	SUSTAINABILITY
Saved about $1.6 million.	None declared by company.	2,098 fewer trucks loads which saves over 1,800 tons of CO_2 annually.

Efficient Fleets & Logistics

Companies are also using more efficient vehicles in their fleets as well as re examining their routing to be more efficient. UPS changed their routing to avoid left turns and to reduce idling. It started using software in 2006 for this purpose and it helped it eliminate 28.5 million delivery miles, saving about 3 million gallons of gas and 31,000 metric tons of would-be greenhouse gas emissions.

Wal-Mart[clxxiv] set a goal to increase the efficiency of its vehicle fleet of more than 7,200 by 25 percent by 2009, and by 50 percent by 2016.

FINANCIAL	BRAND	SUSTAINABILITY
Saves $35 million to $50 million per year. Total savings by 2010 projected at 28–30% of 2005 transportation costs.	Customers and suppliers know that as fuel prices continue to rise, Wal-Mart is doing its part.	This will lead to a subsequent reduction of the fleets' carbon emission, by about 28–30%.

Sourcing Locally

Wal-Mart[clxxv]expanded peach purchasing from a few suppliers to buying from farms in 18 states.

FINANCIAL	BRAND	SUSTAINABILITY
$1.4 million in annual savings.	Allows Wal-Mart to engage with the growing segment of consumers who are demanding local food.	Saves about 100,000 gallons of diesel fuel annually and eliminates 672,000 food miles, reducing CO_2 emissions accordingly.

Material Recovery & Industrial Ecology

Many companies have developed new revenue sources from materials they used to throw out. Initiating product material recovery programs and finding opportunities to sell waste from business operations to other companies can lower disposal costs, create additional revenue streams on the income statement, and reduce carbon emissions.

One example of a group helping businesses do this is Product Synergy Northwest, which helps Northwest companies work together to identify and implement "synergies" that allow one company's waste to become another company's resource. This is based off the process developed by the US Business Council for Sustainable Development.

Many companies have found ways to use product waste in other products.

Andersen Corporation[clxxvi]

This company took wood waste from its manufacturing process and developed a composite material that it now uses to produce some of its windows and doors.

FINANCIAL	BRAND	SUSTAINABILITY
Expected to yield a 50% return on investment	Able to market a composite material to its more environmentally concerned customers	Decreased solid lumber purchases by 750,000 board-feet, which keeps trees sequestrating carbon instead of releasing it upon harvest

Ben and Jerry's and Starbucks[clxxvii]

To reduce their impact on the environment, Ben & Jerry's began using its ice cream waste to feed pigs being raised on a farm in Stowe, Vermont..

Starbucks also thought creatively about how to dispose of its old coffee grounds. Now, anyone can go to any Seattle Starbucks coffee shop and pick up leftover coffee grounds to use in their garden. This is a way Starbucks thought creatively about how to reduce disposal costs and act in a more sustainable manner.

Product Take-Back Programs

Kodak has an extensive take-back program that recovers 70% of all of its cameras sold and recycles or reuses more than 85% of the materials in each new camera.[clxxviii] This has significantly reduced Kodak's cost of goods sold.[clxxix] A number of computer and electronics companies offer "e-waste" take-back programs, including Dell, HP, Apple, Sony, and Toshiba, which now take back most major computer components.[clxxx] Outdoor apparel company Patagonia takes back long underwear and other polypropylene-based textiles for recycling.

Another take-back–type program is product leasing. Interface, a carpet company, pioneered this model with its recycled, non-toxic carpet tiles. Instead of buying carpet, companies lease the carpet tiles, and when the tiles get stained or worn out, the company just swaps out the bad tiles for new ones rather than having to replace the entire carpet. This saves on purchasing, installation, maintenance, and disposal costs; and obviously is less hassle for the office. Taking it a step further, Interface reclaims the tiles at the end of their lives to be recycled and made into new tiles. This is an especially valuable service to companies that want to reduce their facility costs and might need to only replace a particular part of their carpet such as those near high-traffic or stain-prone areas.

Moreover, if companies still do not see the opportunities in a material recovery program, know that regulation might require them to do so. Several states, including California, Connecticut, Maine, Maryland, Minnesota, New Jersey, North Carolina, Oregon, Texas, and Washington, have passed major e-waste recycling legislation.[clxxxi] Arkansas, Massachusetts, Montana, New Hampshire, and Rhode Island have all passed disposal bans or studies related to e-waste.

Conclusion

Supply chain managers have had the traditional role of devising the fastest, most efficient and cost-effective way to deliver their goods or services at the highest possible quality.[clxxxii] Adding climate and sustainability considerations will increasingly be part of supply chain strategies, and as the above examples demonstrate, supply chain efficiency and sustainability are related goals. Companies that want to succeed through this century will have to incorporate sustainability strategies into their supply chains or will eventually find themselves at a competitive disadvantage in a marketplace increasingly shaped by climate change.

CHAPTER 11

MARKETING TO GREEN CONSUMERS

Consumers, lenders, and decision makers were all thrown for a loop when the 2008 financial crisis challenged Americans faith in US corporations. They want to spend and deposit their money with companies they trust, think will be around for a while, and share their values. To this point, a groundswell of research shows that consumers are increasingly showing a preference for more sustainable products and services, and these values are reflected in their purchasing decisions.

This chapter explains how during a time when retailers and service providers are cutting prices and market differentiation is harder than ever, opportunities exist for companies to attract new customers, increase customer loyalty, generate positive publicity, and help insulate themselves against potential public relations nightmares by having climate friendly products and services.

The Lifestyles of Health and Sustainability (LOHAS) Market

According to the brand strategy firm Lippincott Mercer, climate change is a significant issue to the majority of consumers, even in the US.[clxxxiii]

Businesses should not ignore this increasingly influential demographic which are known as green, climate-conscious, ethical, or LOHAS consumers. Quite the contrary, they should move quickly to embrace it. An estimated 16% of the US population (35 million people) is considered LOHAS consumers, and the $209 billion US marketplace they create is characterized by a range of goods and services focused on health, the environment, social justice, personal development, and sustainable living.[clxxxiv]

LOHAS Market Sectors

Sustainable Economy Green Building and Industrial Tools Renewable Energy Resource Efficient Products Socially Responsible Investing Alternative Transportation Environmental Management *US Market--$76.47 billion*	**Healthy Lifestyles** Natural, organics; nutritional products Food and beverage Dietary supplements Personal Care *US Market--$30 billion*
Alternative Healthcare Health and wellness solutions Acupuncture, homeopathy, naturopathy Holistic disease prevention Complementary medicine *US Market--$30.7 billion*	**Personal development** Mind, body and spirit products such as cds, books, tapes, seminars Yoga, fitness, weight loss Spirtual products and services *US Market--$10.63 billion*
Ecological Lifestyles Ecological home and office products Organic/recycled fiber products Environmentally-friendly appliances Eco-tourism and travel *US Market--$81.19 billion*	

Figure 32. The five LOHAS market sectors. [clxxxv]

Companies concerned with meeting the demands of this growing segment of consumers must fully understand these consumers, what their values are, and identify opportunities to meet their needs. There is huge money to be made by delivering goods and services to this market space, especially because consumer awareness and concern about climate change is only expected to grow.

"Sustainable" or "Conscious" Consumers?

A study by the marketing firm BBMG found that nearly nine in ten Americans believe that the words "conscious consumer" describe them well.

Desired Company Practices

Commit to environmentally-friendly practices	87%
Support fair labor and trade practices	87%
Promote health and safety benefits	88%
Manufacture energy efficient products	90%

Figure 33. Desired company practices of "conscious consumers."

Supporting this argument, Jeffrey Pollock, president of Global Strategy Group, said that "many consumers tend to prefer to buy from companies that reflect their values and are increasingly likely to buy from companies that demonstrate they are good for people and the planet."[clxxxvi]

> "In a few years there will be no such thing as green marketing or climate marketing because we're all going to have to be marketing that way, in one way or another." —Marty McDonald, egg[l]

We have entered a new era in which consumers are educated about environmental and social issues and are empowered with information about companies at unprecedented levels. The result is the advent of a new type of consumer: one who cares about taking care of the Earth for future generations, expects companies to be responsible corporate citizens, and votes with their wallet accordingly.

> "Managers ought to begin their deliberations about the ethical impact of marketing activities on society with this fundamental dictum of "people first" as their guide if they hope to prosper in the long run." —Laczniak and Murphy 2006[m]

Whether or not a product is environmentally and socially responsible has become the tiebreaker after quality, performance, and price and is a central concern when consumers are choosing which product to buy. Another study, by Edelman, found that these attributes have moved into the forefront of the consumer decision process. In fact, as business looks to attract the next generation of consumers and employees, this is truer than ever:

- College students ranked social responsibility more important than celebrity endorsement for brand.[clxxxvii]

- 80% of teens are concerned about the environment and the role of the US in causing pollution.[clxxxviii]

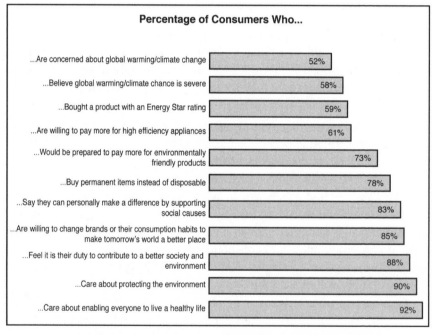

Figure 34. Consumers are concerned about sustainability issues.[clxxxix, cxc]

This chart is important because one targeted way to simultaneously address all of these issues is through a proactive climate change strategy.

Opportunities

Leading companies are strategically positioning themselves to capitalize on this growing green market sector. To create an effective marketing campaign that develops trust and credibility, companies must be authentic in their work and claims to avoid accusations of "green washing," which is a term used for companies that overhype the environmental benefits of their products or services.

Consumers are savvy and will see through slick attempts to paint a picture of a product or service that claims to be more green or sustainable than it truly is. Therefore it is important to first establish a sustainability initiative first and *then* consider how to generate publicity and to communicate this information to consumers.

There has been an explosion in the number of publications rating business on their green, or sustainability performance recently. As you can

> "Sustainability is an innovation and productivity engine waiting to be turned on. Wise executives have the key." —Bob Willard[n]

see from this 2007 comparison that Sustainable Business Consulting created (Figure 35), companies are being evaluated in far more categories than in the past, making it easier for consumers to support companies that share their values and simultaneously harder for companies to hide their true impacts of their products or services.

Company Name	Global 100 Most Sustainable Corp.	Fortune 100 Best US Co. to Work For	Fortune 20 Most Admired US Co.	Sustain-ability Global Reporters Rankings	Business Ethics Magazine 100 Best Corporate Citizens	Natural Marketing Institute LOHAS Index 2007	Total
Google	X	X	X		X		4
Microsoft		X	X		X	X	4
Nike	X	X		X	X		4
Starbucks		X	X	X	X		4
Goldman Sachs	X	X	X				3
Intel	X			X	X		3
Nordstrom		X	X		X		3
PepsiCo			X		X	X	3
United Parcel Service			X		X	X	3
Whole Foods Market		X			X	X	3

Figure 35. Company performance on popular sustainability indices, 2007.

The table compares companies across a number of sustainability measures to create a detailed comparison of their performance. The full comparison of the top 50 companies is in Appendix C.

Reduced Exposure to NGO Attacks

Companies that take real and significant steps to improve their climate impacts and deliver products and services to this new green and climate-conscious consumer will also realize the additional benefit of reduced exposure to attacks from NGOs.

Sustainability Initatives + Marketing = Enhanced Brand Value

We've all known companies that have tried to do the right thing, only to then be lambasted by environmental groups for not doing enough. Consumer advocates know when sustainability is being used as a PR stunt rather than reflecting a genuine shift in corporate operations. It is therefore critical for companies to have their ducks in a row before marketing their sustainability initiatives. Here are a few examples of companies that have reduced their exposure to NGO attacks through enhanced sustainability performance.

General Electric

The company launched its Ecomagination campaign in May 2005 to increase its investment in clean technology research, grow revenues of green products, reduce GHG emissions, and keep the public informed of its progress. This has dramatically helped its brand value because prior to this time, GE had been hammered about its environmental performance, especially around the issue of it dumping polychlorinated biphenyls (PCBs) into the Hudson River.

FINANCIAL	BRAND	SUSTAINABILITY
Revenues from the sale of energy-efficient and environmentally advanced products and services were $12 billion in 2006, up 20% from 2005.	Since the launch of Ecomagination, GE has consistently been rated as one of the top sustainable businesses in the US and has received millions of dollars in free publicity, insulating itself against attacks.	The products it is offering around Ecomagination, such as wind power and energy efficiency help to diversify US energy sources.

Wal-Mart

Consistently criticized by the media and public interest groups for its poor social and environmental policies, Wal-Mart launched a comprehensive sustainability initiative in October 2005, setting bold goals for everything from energy and climate change to supply chain management.

FINANCIAL	BRAND	SUSTAINABILITY
Sold more than 100 million CFLs in less than one year. Achieved 15% improvement in building efficiency, saving thousands in reduced energy costs annually.	Wal-Mart went from being a company that every environmental group attacked to one that people began to highlight for its good work.	The company has begun influencing 60,000 suppliers to improve environmental aspects of their products. It also dramatically impacted the textile industry as it became the single largest purchaser of organic cotton.

BP

Starting in 2000, BP began aggressively communicating its environmental values through its Beyond Petroleum initiative. This paid off dramatically in the spring of 2006, when BP was responsible for one of the largest oil spill in the history of the Prudhoe Bay oil field on Alaska's North Slope.

FINANCIAL	BRAND	SUSTAINABILITY
The company was able to avoid lengthy and costly lawsuits, unlike Exxon, which racked up billions in legal costs associated with its 1989 Valdez oil spill. This spill was much smaller, but BP avoided huge costs.	BP's well-established sustainability initiative, combined with an immediate and comprehensive clean-up, turned what could have been a brand nightmare into a low-profile news story. BP avoided a major PR crisis and is still listed by the World Business Council for Sustainable Development as one of the most sustainable firms in the world.	BP took the action seriously and changed its inspection practices to ensure against future spills along the pipeline in Alaska's fragile wilderness.

Conclusion

More and more consumers are choosing products and services that align with their social, environmental, and climate values. As this trend continues, the companies that meet the needs of these consumers will come to dominate the marketplace, while those that fail to communicate their sustainability values will fall away.

To stay competitive, and to reap the vast financial and brand benefits that are out there in the market, companies would be wise to address the new consumer reality and integrate sustainability into their products, services, operations, and supply chains, and be sure to market it effectively and authentically to their customer base.

CHAPTER 12

CORPORATE SOCIAL RESPONSIBILITY REPORTING

The debate about CSR, the responsibility that businesses have to their workers, and to the communities and environments in which they operate, is as old as business itself. Recently this debate has been reinvigorated through the advent of CSR reporting, which is the modern model for ethical business protocol.

Although it is still in its emergent phase, CSR reporting is something that most businesses will need to do soon. This is especially true as consumers and stakeholders increasingly demand action on climate change and seek transparency after the fallout from the 2008 economic crisis. I believe that this will result in more pressure on business leaders to perform CSR reporting just as the Enron and WorldCom scandals of 2001 led to enhanced financial reporting procedures due to Sarbanes-Oxley.

The presence of numerous reporting schemes and industry-specific methodologies has made it challenging for business leaders to determine the best way to navigate through this new type of reporting.

Therefore, in this chapter I provide a summary of recent CSR trends and highlight the different certification standards that businesses may need to comply with in the coming years.[cxci]

Trends

Before I get into the details of the various CSR methodologies, it is important to describe several major trends that are beginning to emerge from this complicated landscape:

- Industry collaboration

- Transparency

- Interest from Wall Street

- A focus on environment and climate

- Standardization

Industry Collaboration for Reporting Standards

There are countless industry-specific codes of conduct, registries, standards, protocols, and certifications that a company could be subjected to or choose to voluntarily participate in as part of their CSR activities. The number of options can be overwhelming, not to mention time-consuming and costly to track, implement, and report. In an effort to streamline and simplify CSR reporting, the creators of these earlier standards are collaborating to create a single standard for all businesses to use, both internally and in comparing performance against industry peers and competitors. This standardization will lower the barriers for companies trying to do this reporting.

Rise in Transparency of Reporting

According to a 2007 study by the SIRAN analyst network, 49% of S&P 100 companies in the US are now issuing comprehensive reports on their social and environmental performance.[cxcii] The frequency and transparency of reporting is expected to continue to increase and may in fact become a standard practice like financial reporting.

Since CSR and GHG emissions reporting are so new, some companies and investors are wary of sharing information ahead of their peers and are concerned about coming under attack from environmental groups and activists. It is true that in some cases, the businesses trying to do the most and be as transparent as possible are the ones that get attacked for not doing enough; however, as more companies pledge to improve their emissions, transparency will become more common practice.

> "Sample CDP Questions
> General Opportunities: How does climate change present general opportunities for your company?
>
> Regulatory Risks: How is your company exposed to regulatory risks related to climate change?
>
> Regulatory Opportunities: How do current or anticipated regulatory requirements on climate change offer opportunities for your company?
>
> Risk Management: Has your company taken or planned action to manage the general and regulatory risks and/or adapt to the physical risks you have identified?
>
> Maximizing Opportunities: Do you invest in, or have plans to invest in products and services that are designed to minimize or adapt to the effects of climate change?

The Carbon Disclosure Project (CDP) is working to reduce the risks associated with transparency by facilitating dialogue and information-sharing between companies. In 2003, the CDP sent a voluntary questionnaire to all Fortune 500 companies in 2003 and 47% of the companies responded. In 2007, when CDP sent out the questionnaire again, the response rate was much higher, at nearly 77%.[cxciii] The 2008 CDP questionnaire (CDP6) was sent out to more than 1,500 companies that varied in scale and include constituents of the Global 500, FTSE 350 and S&P 500 indices. Together these companies represent close to $57 trillion in assets.

Increasing Attention from Wall Street and Investors

Wall Street and average investors are increasingly looking to company CSR reports. I touched on this in the finance chapter as banks, venture capitalists, and investment firms are all now asking companies about the risks and opportunities that climate change poses to shareholder value and investment portfolios. This makes CSR reporting a very powerful tool for companies and investment firms of all sizes, as it gives companies the opportunity to highlight both the positive steps they are already taking and their plans for future improvement, and it gives potential investors access to the information they can't find in traditional Annual Reports. As more and more companies publicize their CSR reports, this use of reporting will become a regular form for communicating valuable information to stakeholders.

Stronger Focus on Environment Rather than Other Aspects of CSR

In the late 1980s and 1990s, most of the attention being given to "CSR type" activities involved issues of human rights and working conditions in factories overseas, especially for the apparel and outdoor industries. As companies improved their practices, and as climate change has now become the cause of the day, the focus has swung back to environmental issues. According to the results of the 2007 McKinsey survey "Assessing the Impact of Societal Issues on Business and Society," the environmental issues, including climate change, are now considered by executives to be among the most important issues that will affect business over the next five years.[cxciv] This is above workplace conditions, governance, ethical marketing, outsourcing, privacy and data security. Companies need to take climate change and CSR reporting seriously.

Standardization

As I stated earlier, the many different types of CSR reporting make it difficult for companies to know which one to use. Fortunately, some have recently begun to emerge as industry standards because of their comprehensive and carefully researched methodologies, popularity and endorsements, and ability to continually incorporate the most up-to-date information on issues of concern. These include the Global Reporting Initiative (GRI), Ceres, ISO 14000 and 26000, the GHG Protocol, and Climate Counts.

Global Reporting Initiative

The GRI is fast becoming the number-one and de facto CSR reporting standard. In fact, for 95% of businesses, if they were going to use one methodology, it would be the GRI. It provides thorough guidelines for report content, quality, and boundaries and has both universal and industry-specific sections. As of 2007, almost 40% of the S&P 100 companies reported their environmental and social performance using GRI, and this number is steadily increasing. [cxcv] A sample of GRI questions is below:

GRI Performance Indicators		
Indicator	**What It Measures**	**Sample Question**
Environmental (EN)	Organization's impacts on living and non-living natural systems, including ecosystems, land, air, and water	EN2: Percentage of materials used that are recycled input materials
Labor Practices and Decent Work (LA)	Labor and work practices based on internationally recognized universal standards	LA14: Ratio of basic salary of men to women by employee category
Human Rights (HR)	Requires organizations to report on the extent to which human rights are considered in investment and supplier/contractor selection practices	HR2: Percentage of significant suppliers and contractors that have undergone screening on human rights and actions taken

Society (SO)	Impacts that organizations have on the communities in which they operate, and how the risks that may arise from interactions with other social institutions are managed and mediated	SO3: Percentage of employees trained in organization's anti-corruption policies and procedures
Product Responsibility (PR)	Aspects of a reporting organization's products and services that directly affect customers—namely, health and safety, information and labeling, marketing, and privacy	PR1: Life cycle stages in which health and safety impacts of products and services are assessed for improvement, and percentage of significant products and services categories subject to such procedures
Economic (EC)	Organization's impacts on the economic conditions of its at local, national, and global levels	EC2: Financial implications and other risks and opportunities for the organization's activities due to climate change

The goal of the GRI is to provide a uniform approach for companies to benchmark their performances against government regulations and business peers in a way that ensures the highest degree of technical quality, credibility, and relevance.[cxcvi] The first version was released in 2000; and in 2006, an updated version was released to better guide companies through the reporting process.[cxcvii] As market conditions change and industry sectors clamor for industry-specific guidance, new components and updates to the GRI are continually created to accommodate business needs and improve ease of use.

Ceres

This national network, which was one of the first to venture into CSR reporting really led the charge in this arena. It concentrates on working with "companies and investors to address sustainability challenges such as climate change" and in "integrating sustainability into capital markets."[cxcviii] Ceres established a ten-point code of conduct that companies voluntarily commit to reporting on corporate environmental activities. Additionally, Ceres publishes many in-depth reports that highlight industry leaders, trends, best practices, and standards that have been widely used by companies, investors, and the public for CSR work. Though much of its recent work has been focused on climate change, Ceres has been recognized for years as a leader in bringing businesses, environmentalists, and public interests together to create mutual benefit. Companies not wanting to follow GRI should consider Ceres.

ISO 26000

The ISO already has a number of published standards that have contributed to corporate responsibility, such as the ISO 9000 series for quality and the 14000 series for environmental management. A new standard, the ISO 26000 series, is scheduled for release in 2010. This series will establish a new set of standards specifically crafted to address issues of social responsibility for organizations of all sectors and sizes in both developed and developing countries.[cxcix,cc] The standards will be internationally focused and, as with most ISO standards, will encourage voluntary commitment. The 26000 series' goal is similar to the GRI in that it is intended to develop a set of common "concepts, definitions and evaluation methods."[cci] This series is of particular importance to international businesses, as many countries will likely require compliance with 26000 just as European countries now require compliance with ISO 14000.

GHG Protocol and ISO 14064

As noted in Chapter 2, the WRI, WBCSD and ISO are now working together to promote their protocols for GHG tracking and reporting. These have become the international standards on which the vast majority of emissions calculators, carbon inventory tools, and GHG inventories are based for governments, schools, non-profits, and businesses. Their coordination will definitely impact and improve CSR reporting in the future.

Climate Counts

Climate Counts, a nonprofit organization, launched its first corporate scorecard in 2007. This organization ranks companies' climate performance relative to their industry competitors and peers. The report is updated annually and includes details on:

- How a company measures GHG emissions

- The plans a company has to reduce GHG emissions

- The company's response to current regulation

- How much information the company presents to the public

"We launched our organization as a proxy for the average consumer. Our 22 criteria scorecard provides climate-conscious consumers with a solid yardstick to compare the climate actions and strategies of the world's largest companies. We're trying to encourage business to innovate when it comes to climate and to see it not just in terms of responsibility and accountability but as opportunity." — Wood Turner, Executive Director, Climate Counts [p]

Sample Climate Counts Questions

How strong is the measurement of the baseline year used for the reduction goal (keeping in mind changes in company's size/composition)?

Have a management plan and organizational structure been established for climate?

Does the company work to educate its employees, trade association, and/or customers on how they can reduce individual GHG emissions (through direct education programs, incentives, or philanthropic projects)?

Is the company publicly reporting on emissions, risks, and actions? How is information disclosed? Company-based (e.g., on their website or annual report) or through a credible third-party program (e.g., CDP, GRI, etc.)?

Does the company require suppliers to take climate change action or give preference to those that do?

Others

There are numerous other standards, certifications, and regulations that involve aspects of CSR (See Appendix D) for various industries, products, and countries. From the Electronic Industry Code of Conduct to the Pharmaceutical Supply Chain Initiative, and from the Fair Trade Labeling Organization to the US EPA's ENERGY STAR program, companies can find many programs to help them define their CSR goals and tap into collaborative efforts to define best practices and support CSR activities. The healthy marketplace of ideas represented by the many initiatives listed above should help companies that are just trying to get started on this process.

Conclusion

Currently there is no single standardized definition or process for CSR reporting but businesses need to be aware that increasingly rigorous and transparent reporting procedures for all business sectors and sizes are becoming more common. Smart business leaders understand that they need to record, track, and improve upon their CSR performance, especially as consumers, suppliers, and stakeholders are demanding greater transparency from the fallout of the financial crisis and also want action on climate change. The good news is that many companies are already incorporating CSR into their core operations and have experienced tangible benefits to their bottom line by doing so.

FINAL THOUGHTS

Addressing climate change is a great challenge but a solvable one, and business must be a part of the solution. Just because we are living in a period of economic uncertainty does not mean we can avoid this responsibility.

Throughout this book, I've attempted to not only highlight the risks of inaction but also provide the ROS methodology to help your company capitalize on the numerous business opportunities that climate change presents. So the next time you are in a meeting or boardroom, and someone says they "can't afford to address climate change" because of "the bottom line," you can no longer just sit back quietly. You must speak up, because you are now armed with practical actions and real-world case studies of companies that have successfully improved their climate performances, enhanced brand value, and increased profitability at the same time.

It is up to us—all of us—to decide if we are going to meet this potential social and environmental catastrophe head-on or if we are going to skirt our responsibility.

As you go about your work in your business, I implore you to recognize that you are not a leader for tomorrow, but a leader for today— for the here and now. Your company, your colleagues, your shareholders—but most importantly, your friends, family, loved ones, and the planet—are counting on you.

Take what you've learned in the previous pages and put it to work within your organization, and join me in taking action toward halting climate change today!

ABOUT MY FIRM: SUSTAINABLE BUSINESS CONSULTING

www.sustainablebizconsulting.com
I envision a world where profitable sustainability is not just a way of doing business but is the ONLY way of doing business. Our mission at SBC is therefore to help companies make more money through sustainable business practices. We are guided in this work by the following set of principles and values.

Our Guiding Principles

- Address climate change head-on—be a part of the solution.

- Be a profitable, diverse, and learning organization.

- Deliver customized client solutions that create extraordinary value through the integration of sustainable practices.

- Create an open, trusting, and forgiving environment, fostering personal and professional growth.

- Collaborate and engage with business, government, and community leaders to accelerate sustainable development.

- Support and encourage a quality life-work balance, volunteerism, and community involvement.

- Encourage continuous improvement in upholding these values and principles.

Our Business Values

- Partnership

- Excellence

- Authenticity

- Fun

Sustainable Business Consulting combines cutting-edge sustainability implementation strategies and expert financial analysis to deliver customized client solutions. We do this not by providing a "one size fits all" approach toward working with clients but by delivering customized practical and actionable solutions to help firms achieve their profitability and sustainability goals.

Life-Work Balance

SBC applies this same personal ethic to the way we run our own business, too. At SBC, we work to live. For us, this means not only fostering a healthy life-work balance but also acknowledging and nurturing the whole person—not just the professional part. Our staff is committed to enhancing the community in which we live through our volunteerism and charitable giving. Additionally, SBC contributes up to 10% of its annual net profit to nonprofit organizations.

SBC offers a full benefits package with generous vacation policy and encourages employees to use it so their time in the office is productive. In addition to vacation days, we offer the following paid holidays: New Year's Eve, New Year's Day, Martin Luther King, Jr. Day, the opening day of the NCAA Basketball Tournament, Memorial Day, July 4th, Labor Day, Yom Kippur, Thanksgiving, and Christmas Day.

Time off may also be allocated for key US soccer and Seattle Sounders matches, as determined by the CEO.

Although Canada Day is not an official paid holiday, we shall pay respect to our northern brothers and sisters by finishing all questions on July 1st with an "eh?"

Each employee receives a half day off for his or her birthday and anniversary, as well as a non-paid half day off the Friday before the Ohio State – Michigan game in order to prepare.

Additionally, SBC provides many resources to help staff succeed in all aspects of their lives. All SBC staff who work more than 24 hours per week receive a range of sustainability-related benefits, such as:

- Health and wellness stipends, as well as an annual flu shot

- Cash bonuses for biking to work, and provision of bus passes to all staff

- Telecommuting option for those working more than 4 days/week

- Purchase of carbon offsets for all staff activity outside of work

- Cash match on personal energy savings initiatives up to $250

- 50 hours paid time off for volunteer service, and company sponsorship for two charitable races or triathlons

- Shared Forest Service, National Parks, and Sno-Park passes for staff and contractor use

- One additional day off per year for skiing or kayaking…but not for snowboarding

SBC Client Services

Carbon Footprinting & Climate-Change Strategy

As this book details, climate change is quickly becoming an issue that all businesses must address. SBC is a recognized leader in helping companies across all sectors successfully address this issue head-on. We understand that whatever actions companies take must also make sense financially, and we'll help your firm find practical, innovative, and cost-effective ways to improve climate performance, brand value, and profitability at the same time.

We believe the best first step in this process is to understand your current baseline impact through a carbon footprint. Once we have conducted this and looked at all of your emissions related to energy, transportation, shipping, materials, and waste, we will help you develop the best plan for reduction.

Additionally, we will ensure that your strategy stays ahead of regulation and industry standards such as those being applied through the debt and equity markets, the insurance industry, and across the supply chain.

- Greenhouse gas inventory, carbon footprint analysis

- Sustainability goal and strategy development

- Detailed analysis of the financial, brand, and sustainability benefit of each action item

- Incentive identification for addressing potential regulations

- Employee engagement: education, awareness, activities, things you can do today

- Corporate climate policy

- Internal and external communication

Business & Financial Case for Sustainability

Profitability is essential to business, and implementation of sustainability goals must ultimately result in positive cash flow. This is why, from simple back-of-the-envelope cost-benefit calculations to a full financial analysis of your firm, Sustainable Business Consulting can perform a range of services for each initiative to ensure it makes business sense and supports financial targets.

- Cost-saving and revenue-generation opportunities

- Return on Sustainability analysis

- Demonstrated profit improvement

- ROI and NPV calculations

- Increased brand value opportunities

Sustainability Implementation

SBC recognizes that the value of a great plan is only realized once the plan is put to action. For this reason, we are committed to getting our clients to start walking their own talk as soon as possible.

- Cost savings through energy efficiency, waste reduction, and process improvement

- Greening your supply chain, products, and services

- Greening your office: Practices to make office operations more sustainable.

- Employee engagement: Workshops and recommendations for engaging and empowering employees to make sustainable choices in their jobs. Green Teams.

Strategic & Business Planning Services

SBC works hand-in-hand with clients to develop their sustainability goals and then maps out the strategy to bring that vision to reality. We don't write plans just to have them sit on a shelf; we want to see them implemented. We also make sure that we match each step with the company's budget so that the plan is realistic and is consistent with cash flow.

Our experience is that incorporating sustainability or climate change into the overall strategy is something new for most clients. The concept is often met with some skepticism at first, which is why it is so important for clients to experience success. We ensure clients achieve early wins by meeting meaningful, cost-effective goals to build momentum for tackling challenges ahead.

- Strategic/business planning and implementation

- Opportunity and feasibility analysis

- Expert cross-discipline business advisory services

- Market penetration and growth strategies

- CSR reporting

Clean Technology Expertise

SBC consults for several renewable energy and clean tech start-ups and is deeply involved in efforts to galvanize and grow targeted clean technology sectors in the Northwest.

In 2008, SBC wrote the strategic plan for the City of Seattle in support of its goal of becoming a national leader in the clean technology industry. We also inventoried all local and national legislation (both enacted and pending) relating to clean technology and climate change for the Puget Sound Regional Council. While tackling these projects and others similar in scope, we typically bring together a diverse body of stakeholders such as:

- Industry executives

- Public officials

- Entrepreneurs

- Angel investors and venture capitalists

- University researchers and representatives

Our firm helps clients develop short- and long-term strategies and recommended action steps to effect change within the clean tech sector with regard to:

- Public policy

- Funding mechanisms

- Research and commercialization

- Business competitiveness

- Workforce development

- Communication

Lastly, SBC has also written and contributed to several industry and policy papers around clean technology, which are available on our website: www.sustainablebizconsulting.com.

GLOSSARY

Cap and Trade: see Emissions Trading

Carbon: Carbon exists in the Earth's atmosphere primarily as the gas carbon dioxide (CO_2). The overall atmospheric concentration of these greenhouse gases has been increasing dramatically since the industrial revolution, contributing to global warming.

Carbon Credit: Carbon credits are components of a tradable permit scheme. They provide a way to reduce greenhouse gas emissions by capping emissions and then giving them a monetary value. One credit gives the owner the right to emit one ton of carbon dioxide.

Carbon Footprint: The carbon footprint is a measure of the exclusive total amount of carbon dioxide emissions that are directly and indirectly caused by an activity (e.g., operating a business) or are accumulated over the life stages of products.

Carbon Neutral: An activity or product is carbon neutral if it has no net greenhouse gas emissions. This can be achieved through reductions in energy consumption, use of renewable sources, offsetting of GHG emissions, or a combination of any or all of these strategies.

Carbon Offsetting: The act of compensating for greenhouse gas emissions. An example of carbon offsetting is financially supporting the construction of a wind farm to make up for the greenhouse gas emissions from personal air travel.

Carbon Project: A business initiative that receives funding because it will reduce greenhouse gas emissions. To demonstrate that the project will result in real, permanent, verifiable reductions in greenhouse gases, proof must be provided in the form of a project design document and activity reports validated by an approved third party.

Carbon Sequestration: A process that removes carbon dioxide from the atmosphere through a variety of means of capturing and storing carbon. Plants and other organisms play a critical role in natural sequestration when they carry out photosynthesis. The oceans and vegetation (including soil) are key CO_2 "sinks."

Chicago Climate Exchange (CCX): The world's first (and North America's only) voluntary, legally binding greenhouse gas reduction and trading system for emission sources and offset projects in North America and Brazil. CCX employs independent verification, includes six greenhouse gases, and has been trading greenhouse gas emission allowances since 2003. The companies joining the exchange commit to reducing their aggregate emissions by 6% by 2010.

Clean Energy: Environmentally friendly sources of energy. Typically, this refers to renewable and nonpolluting energy sources.

Climate Change: Variations in the Earth's climate over time. The dominant mechanisms to which recent climate change has been attributed all result from human activity. They include the following:

Increasing atmospheric concentrations of greenhouse gases
Global changes to land surface, such as deforestation
Increasing atmospheric concentrations of aerosols.

CO_2: Carbon dioxide

CO_2 Equivalent: The conversion of the global warming potential of each of the six greenhouse gases to a CO_2 equivalent or CO_2e.

Corporate Social Responsibility (CSR): A concept that encourages organizations to consider the interests of society by taking responsibility for the impact of the organization's activities on customers, employees, shareholders, communities, and environment in all aspects of their operations. Decisions are then based on the short- and long-term social and environmental consequences as well as financial factors such as profits or dividends.

Ecological Footprint: A methodology to measure human demand on nature by comparing rates of human consumption of natural resources with Earth's ecological capacity to regenerate them and absorb the corresponding wastes. Using this assessment, it is possible to estimate how many Earths it would take to support humanity if everybody lived a given lifestyle.

Ecosystem Services: All the myriad resources and functions provided by natural ecosystems from which humanity benefits and on which civilization has come to depend. The quantity and variety of ecosystem services are immense and range from the photosynthesis of crops to creation of clean drinking water. An oft-cited value for these services is estimated to be $33 billion.

Energy Development: The ongoing effort to provide sustainable energy resources. Primary considerations include climate change, oil depletion, renewable energy implementation, population growth, and an increase in per capita consumption levels.

Environmental Sustainability: The ability of the Earth's ecosystems to continue to function properly indefinitely. The goal of environmental sustainability is to eliminate systematic environmental degradation by using natural resources at a rate that doesn't exceed nature's ability to replenish them. See also Sustainable Development.

Emissions Factor (Emissions Coefficient): The average emission rate of a given pollutant for a given source, relative to units of activity. For example, combusting one gallon of gasoline releases about 19.56 pounds of carbon dioxide on average. Thus, the emissions coefficient for gasoline is 19.56 lbs. CO_2/gal. Emissions factors are essential in developing national, regional, state, and local emissions inventories for air quality management decisions and in developing emissions-control strategies.

Emissions Trading: An administrative approach used to control pollution by setting a limit or cap on the amount of the pollutant that can be emitted. Companies that emit the pollutant are given *credits* that represent the right to emit a specific amount. Companies that pollute beyond their allowances must buy credits from others who pollute less than their allowances or face heavy penalties. Emissions Trading is commonly referred to as Cap and Trade.

Environment, Social, Governance (ESG): Bank of America's commitment to considering environmental, social, and governance issues into its selection criteria.

Global Warming: The unnatural warming of the Earth's climate. Since the advent of the Industrial Revolution in the 1700s, humans have devised many inventions that burn fossil fuels such as coal, oil, and natural gas. Burning these fossil fuels, as well as other activities such as clearing land for agriculture or urban settlements, releases greenhouse gases, which have now risen to levels higher than at any time in at least the last 650,000 years. As these gases build up in the atmosphere, they trap more heat near Earth's surface, causing Earth's climate to become warmer than it would naturally.

Global Reporting Initiative (GRI): The Global Reporting Initiative is the world's de facto standard for sustainability reporting guidelines. Sustainability reporting is the public communication by an organization of its economic, environmental, and social performance.

Greenhouse Gases (GHGs): Greenhouse gases are components of the atmosphere that contribute to the greenhouse effect, which leads to climate change by warming global temperatures. Greenhouse gases include carbon dioxide, methane, nitrous oxide, ozone, and water vapor. The main six that you will track as a company are Carbon Dioxide, Nitrous Oxide, Methane, Sulfur Hexafluoride, Hydrofluorocarbons, and Perfluorocarbons.

Greenhouse Gas Protocol: The most widely accepted standard for calculating GHG emissions. The two main components of the Protocol are Corporate Accounting and Reporting Standards (methodologies for business and other organizations to inventory and report all of the GHG emissions they produce) and Project Accounting Protocol and Guidelines (geared toward calculating reductions in GHG emissions from specific GHG-reduction projects).

Green Tags: See Renewable Energy Certificates.

Green Washing: The unjustified appropriation of environmental virtue by a company, an industry, a government, a politician, or even a nongovernment organization to create a pro-environmental image, sell a product or a policy, or try to rehabilitate its standing with the public and decision makers after being embroiled in controversy.

Greenhouse Effect: The capacity of certain gases in the atmosphere to trap heat emitted from Earth's surface, thereby insulating and warming the planet. Without the thermal blanketing of the natural greenhouse effect, Earth's climate would be about 33°C (about 59°F) cooler—too cold for most living organisms to survive. Scientists are growing increasingly concerned that human activities may be modifying this natural process, with potentially dangerous consequences.

HVAC: An acronym that stands for "heating, ventilation, and air conditioning." Because HVAC systems control the interior climate of buildings, they can play a key role in reducing energy costs as well as anthropogenic contributions to global warming.

Industrial Ecology: An industrial system that is compatible with the way natural ecosystems function. Industrial ecology understands ___ interactions with the biosphere, and uses the waste from one process as the raw material for others. Energy and materials are optimized, wastes and pollution are minimized, and every product of the manufacturing process is economically viable.[ccii, cciii]

Kyoto Protocol: An international agreement by which signatory nations agree to reduce greenhouse gas emissions. As of December 2007, a total of 174 countries and other governmental entities have ratified the agreement. The United States and Kazakhstan are the only major emitters of greenhouse gases that have not ratified the Protocol. The Protocol calls for countries to reduce their greenhouse gas emissions by a collective average of 5% below their 1990 levels.

LED (Light Emitting Diode): LED is a technology used in light bulbs. LEDs use 80–90% less energy than incandescent bulbs, produce very little heat, and can last 100,000 hours or more. For these reasons, they compare very favorably with incandescent or compact fluorescent bulbs, despite their higher up-front costs.

Leadership in Energy and Environmental Design (LEED): A green building rating system developed by the U.S. Green Building Council that provides a suite of standards for environmentally sustainable construction. There are four levels: Certified, Silver, Gold, and Platinum.

Lean Manufacturing: A business practice that emphasizes eliminating waste in manufacturing processes.

Life Cycle Assessment (LCA): The assessment of the environmental impact of a given product or service throughout its lifespan. The goal of LCA is to enable the comparison of the environmental performance of products and services. The procedures of LCA are part of the ISO 14000 environmental management standards.

$MTCO_2e$: Metric ton of Carbon Dioxide (CO_2) equivalent.

Net Metering: A state-level electricity policy for consumers who own "qualifying facilities," which are generally smaller renewable energy sources such as a wind or solar power. Under net metering, an individual or organization can receive retail credit for at least a portion of the electricity they generate and feed back to the grid.

Peak Oil: The point in time at which the maximum global petroleum production rate is reached, where demand passes supply and the rate of production enters a terminal decline.

Pound of CO_2: A measure of carbon dioxide emission. Watching 1 hour of television releases ½ pound of CO_2. **Renewable Energy Certificate (REC):** The property rights to the environmental benefits from generating electricity from renewable energy sources (i.e., how many tons of greenhouse gases are *not* released). RECs are also referred to as Green Tags, Renewable Energy Credits, or Tradable Renewable Certificates (TRCs).

Renewable Energy Credits: See Renewable Energy Certificates.

Renewable Portfolio Standards: A regulatory policy that requires the increased production of renewable energy sources such as wind, solar, biomass, and geothermal. An example is Washington's successful Initiative 937, which requires electric utilities with more than 25,000 customers to obtain 15% of their electricity from new renewable resources by 2020.

Social Responsibility: A concept whereby an entity, whether it is state, government, corporation, or organization, considers the interests of society by taking responsibility for the impact of its activities on customers, employees, shareholders, communities, and the environment in all aspects of its operations.

Social Venture Capital: Social venture capital provides early-stage investments in companies that have identified profitable ways to meet societal needs—such as water purification or renewable energy technologies—before the companies' stocks are publicly traded

Sustainable Building: The practice of increasing the efficiency of buildings and their use of energy, water, and materials, and reducing building impacts on human health and the environment, through better sighting, design, construction, operation, maintenance, and removal—the complete building life cycle.

Sustainable Development: Balancing the fulfillment of human needs with the protection of the natural environment so that these needs can be met not only in the present but also in the indefinite future.

Sustainable Design: Design with the goal to produce buildings, products, and services in a way that eliminates systematic environmental and social degradation. Sustainable Design may also be referred to as Green Design, Eco-Design or Design for Environment.

Tradable Renewable Certificates (TRCs): See Renewable Energy Certificates.

Volatile Organic Compounds (VOC): Organic chemical compounds that, when released into the environment, can pollute the air, soil, and groundwater. Common sources of VOCs include paint thinners, dry-cleaning solvents, and some constituents of petroleum fuels (e.g., gasoline and natural gas).

World Resources Institute (WRI): WRI helps develop and promote policies with the intention of protecting the Earth and improving people's lives by providing objective information and practical proposals for policy and institutional change that will foster environmentally sound, socially equitable development.

APPENDIX A

EQUATOR PRINCIPLES FINANCIAL INSTITUTIONS

Equator Principles Financial Institutions will only provide loans to projects that conform to Principles 1–9 below:

Principle 1	Review and Categorization	When a project is proposed for financing, the EPFI will, categorize such a project based on the magnitude of its potential impacts and risks in accordance with the environmental and social screening criteria of the IFC.
Principle 2	Social and Environmental Assessment	For each project assessed as being either Category A or Category B, the borrower has conducted a Social and Environmental Assessment process the relevant social and environmental impacts and risks of the proposed project.
Principle 3	Applicable Social and Environmental Standards	For projects located in non-OECD countries, and those located in OECD countries not designated as High-Income, as defined by the World Bank Development Indicators Database, the

Principle 3 *Cont'd*		Assessment will refer to the then applicable IFC Performance Standards.
Principle 4	Action Plan and Management System	For All Category A and Category B projects located in non-OECD countries, and those located in OECD countries not designated as High-Income, the borrower has prepared an Action Plan which addresses the relevant findings and draws on the conclusions of the Assessment. The AP will describe and prioritize the actions needed to implement mitigation measures, corrective actions and monitoring measures necessary to manage the impacts and risks identified in the Assessment.
Principle 5	Consultation and Disclosure	For all Category A, and as appropriate, Category B projects above, the government, borrower or third party expert has consulted with project affected communities in a structured and culturally appropriate manner.
Principle 6	Grievance Mechanism	For all projects listed above, the borrower will establish a grievance mechanism as part of the management system.
Principle 7	Independent Review	For all projects above, an independent social or environmental expert not directly associated with the borrower will review the Assessment and AP.

Principle 8	Covenants	An important strength of the Principles is the incorporation of covenants linked to compliance.
Principle 9	Independent Monitoring and Reporting	EPFIs will require appointment of an independent environmental and/or social expert, or require that the borrower retain qualified and experienced external experts to verify its monitoring information which would be shared with EPFIs.
Principle 10	EPFI Reporting	Each EPFI adopting the Equator Principles commits to report publicly at least annually about its Equator Principles implementation processes and experience, taking into account appropriate confidentiality consideration.

APPENDIX B

UNITED NATIONS PRINCIPLES FOR RESPONSIBLE INVESTMENT

Goal	Possible Actions
Incorporate ESG issues into investment analysis and decision-making processes	<ul><li>Address ESG issues in investment policy statements</li><li>Support development of ESG-related tools, metrics, and analyses</li><li>Ask investment service providers (such as financial analysts, consultants, brokers, research firms, or rating companies) to integrate ESG factors into evolving research and analysis</li><li>Advocate ESG training for investment professionals</li></ul>
Be active owners and incorporate ESG issues into ownership policies and practices	<ul><li>Develop and disclose an active ownership policy consistent with the Principles</li><li>Exercise voting rights or monitor compliance with voting policy (if outsourced)</li><li>Develop an engagement capability (either directly or through outsourcing)</li></ul>

	• Participate in the development of policy, regulation, and standard setting (such as promoting and protecting shareholder rights)
	• File shareholder resolutions consistent with long-term ESG considerations
Seek appropriate disclosure on ESG issues by the entities invested	• Ask for standardized reporting on ESG issues (using tools such as the Global Reporting Initiative)
	• Ask for ESG issues to be integrated within annual financial reports
	• Ask for information from companies regarding adoption of/adherence to relevant norms, standards, codes of conduct or international initiatives (such as the UN Global Compact)
	• Support shareholder initiatives and resolutions promoting ESG disclosure
Promote acceptance and implementation of the Principles within the investment industry	• Include Principles-related requirements in requests for proposals (RFPs)
	• Align investment mandates, monitoring procedures, performance indicators and incentive structures accordingly (for example, ensure investment management processes reflect long-term time horizons when appropriate)
	• Support the development of tools for benchmarking ESG integration
	• Support regulatory or policy developments that enable implementation of the Principles
Work together to enhance effectiveness in implementing the Principles	• Support/participate in networks and information platforms to share tools, pool resources, and make use of investor reporting as a source of learning

Report on activities and progress towards implementing the Principles

- Collectively address relevant emerging issues
- Disclose how ESG issues are integrated within investment practices
- Disclose active ownership activities (voting, engagement, and/or policy dialogue)
- Disclose what is required from service providers in relation to the Principles
- Communicate with beneficiaries about ESG issues and the Principles
- Report on progress and/or achievements relating to the Principles using a 'Comply or Explain approach

APPENDIX C

COMPARISON OF BUSINESSES ACROSS VARIOUS SUSTAINABILITY RANKINGS 2007

Company Name	Global 100 Most Sustainable Corp.[cciv]	Fortune 100 Best US Co. to Work For[ccv]	Fortune 20 Most Admired US Co.[ccvi]	Sustain-Ability Global Reporters Rankings[ccvii]	Business Ethics Magazine 100 Best Corporate Citizens[ccviii]	Natural Marketing Institute LOHAS Index 2007[ccix]	Total
Google	x	x	x		x		4
Microsoft		x	x		x	x	4
Nike	x	x		x	x		4
Starbucks		x	x	x	x		4
Goldman Sachs	x	x	x				3
Intel	x			x	x		3
Nordstrom		x	x		x		3
PepsiCo			x		x	x	3
United Parcel Service			x		x	x	3

Company Name	Global 100 Most Sustainable Corp.[cciv]	Fortune 100 Best US Co. to Work For[ccv]	Fortune 20 Most Admired US Co.[ccvi]	Sustain-Ability Global Reporters Rankings[ccvii]	Business Ethics Magazine 100 Best Corporate Citizens[ccviii]	Natural Marketing Institute LOHAS Index 2007[ccix]	Total
Whole Foods Market		x			x	x	3
3M			x	x	x		2
General Electric	x	x		x			2
Proctor & Gamble		x	x	x			2
ABN AMRO	x			x			2
Adidas	x			x			2
Adobe Systems		x			x		2
Advanced Micro Devices	x				x		2
Agilent Technologies	x				x		2
Alcan	x			x			2
American Express		x			x		2
Astra-Zeneca		x		x			2
BASF	x			x			2
Baxter International	x				x		2
Bright Horizons		x			x		2
British	x			x			2

Company Name	Global 100 Most Sustainable Corp.[cciv]	Fortune 100 Best US Co. to Work For[ccv]	Fortune 20 Most Admired US Co.[ccvi]	Sustain-Ability Global Reporters Rankings[ccvii]	Business Ethics Magazine 100 Best Corporate Citizens[ccviii]	Natural Marketing Institute LOHAS Index 2007[ccix]	Total
Land							
BT	x			x			2
CDW		x			x		2
Cisco Systems		x			x		2
Daiwa Securities Group	x			x			2
Dexia	x			x			2
Eastman Kodak	x				x		2
First Horizon National		x			x		2
Gap				x	x		2
Genzyme	x	x					2
Henkel	x			x			2
Hewlett-Packard	x			x			2
HSBC	x			x			2
Jones Lang LaSalle		x			x		2
Kellogg Company					x	x	2
Kesko	x			x			2
Lafarge	x			x			2
Network Appliance		x			x		2
Novo	x			x			2

Company Name	Global 100 Most Sustainable Corp.[cciv]	Fortune 100 Best US Co. to Work For[ccv]	Fortune 20 Most Admired US Co.[ccvi]	Sustain-Ability Global Reporters Rankings[ccvii]	Business Ethics Magazine 100 Best Corporate Citizens[ccviii]	Natural Marketing Institute LOHAS Index 2007[ccix]	Total
Nordisk							
Philips Electronics	x			x			2
Pricewaterhouse Coopers		x		x			2
Principal Financial Group		x			x		2
SAS Institute		x		x			2
Severn Trent	x			x			2
Shell	x			x			2
Southwest Airlines			x		x		2
Storebrand	x			x			2
Swiss Reinsurance	x			x			2
Texas Instruments		x			x		2
Timberland		x			x		2
Toyota Motor	x		x				2
Unilever	x			x			2
Walt Disney Company	x					x	2
Alcoa Inc.	x						1
Berkshire			x				1

Company Name	Global 100 Most Sustainable Corp.[cciv]	Fortune 100 Best US Co. to Work For[ccv]	Fortune 20 Most Admired US Co.[ccvi]	Sustain- Ability Global Reporters Rankings[ccvii]	Business Ethics Magazine 100 Best Corporate Citizens[ccviii]	Natural Marketing Institute LOHAS Index 2007[ccix]	Total
Hathaway							
Chevron				x			1
Deere & Co					x		1
Exxon Mobil				x			1
Ford				x			1
Kimberly-Clark					x		1
Nucor					x		1
United Technologies Corp.	x						1
Valero Energy		x					1

APPENDIX D

CSR STANDARDS & CERTIFICATIONS

Certification or Standard	Type	Description	How Widely Used
Global Reporting Initiative	Reporting	"Guidance on how companies can disclose their sustainability performance"	> 1000 organization use these standards world-wide
ISO 26000	Social Responsibility	"International Standard providing guidelines for social responsibility"	In development with target release of 2010
Energy Star	Energy	"Help individuals and organizations nationwide adopt cost-effective, energy-efficient technologies and practices and better manage their energy costs." Includes a labeling program.	Over 9,000 business and organizational partners in the US
GHG Protocol	Climate	"Provides standards and guidance for companies and other organizations preparing a GHG	Widely used by thousands of businesses and organizations and as the

Certification or Standard	Type	Description	How Widely Used
		emissions inventory."	foundation for GHG programs and registries globally.
Carbon Disclosure Project	Climate	Collects information on companies' climate risks and opportunities and creates dialogue between investors and companies about addressing climate change.	385 investment firms are signatories to the CDP and thousands of major companies world-wide participate in the annual CDP survey.
Climate Counts	Climate	"Annually updated scorecard reflects the self-reported efforts of companies to address climate change"	60 key US companies across a variety of sectors are rated
LEED	Building	"LEED Green Building Rating System is the nationally accepted benchmark for the design, construction and operation of high-performance green buildings."	Thousands of certified projects globally with projects currently in process in 41 countries.
Design for the Environment (DfE)	Product and Process Design	US EPA program using chemical assessment tools and expertise to "reduce risk to people and the environment by	Has impacted more than 200,000 business facilities.

Certification or Standard	Type	Description	How Widely Used
		preventing pollution." Includes a labeling program.	
MBDC Cradle to Cradle	Product and Process Design	"MBDC's Design Paradigm models human industry on natural processes, creating safe and healthy prosperity." Products that meet materials, material reutilization, energy, water and social responsibility standards may be MBDC certified.	About 40 companies have certified products.
ISO 14000	Environmental Management	These process focused standards are designed to help organizations control their environmental impact, and improve environmental performance through a systematic approach.	Thousands of companies worldwide use the ISO 14000 process.
Fair Trade	Supply Chain - Food and Goods	Standards and labeling system for goods, primarily food products, produced cooperatively with set standards for environmental and	Thousands of producers worldwide sell certified products. A number of major US corporations now carry these

Certification or Standard	Type	Description	How Widely Used
		community impacts, as well as producer wages.	products.
Electronic Industry Code of Conduct (EICC)	Supply Chain - Electronics	"Outlines standards to ensure that working conditions in the electronics industry supply chain are safe, that workers are treated with respect and dignity, and that manufacturing processes are environmentally responsible."	At least 15 major electronics companies are partners including Cisco, IBM, HP and Microsoft.
Pharmaceutical Supply Chain Initiative (PSCI)	Supply Chain - Pharmaceuticals	Shared vision of "improved conditions for workers, economic development and a cleaner environment for local communities." The principles "address five areas of responsible business practices: ethics, labor, health and safety, environment and related management systems."	Seven current members are all major pharmaceutical companies and include Johnson & Johnson, Merck and Novartis.
Suppliers Ethical Data Exchange	Supply Chain – Labor Standards	"Secure, web-based system for companies to input data on labor	Used by over 12,000 factories and 100 retailers and companies

Certification or Standard	Type	Description	How Widely Used
		standards at their production sites." A way to share practices and manage ethical data.	worldwide.
Fair Factories Clearinghouse	Supply Chain – Labor Standards	"Global database of factory information and social compliance audit reports for…sharing non-competitive information about workplace conditions."	Involves retail and consumer brands and retail trade associations. Database contains over 13,000 factories.

APPENDIX E

INTERVIEW AND TEXT BOX REFERENCES

INTERVIEW REFERENCES

Chapter 1: Interview with KC Golden, Policy Director—Climate Solutions. February 4, 2008.

Chapter 2: Interview with Kevin Hagen, CSR Manager—REI. February 11, 2008.

Chapter 3: Interview with Steve Leahy, President—Greater Seattle Chamber of Commerce. February 21, 2008.

Chapter 3: Interview with Bill Beckley, Environmental Consultant Ridolfi, Inc. August 21, 2008.

Chapter 3: Interview with Gifford Pinchot, President—Bainbridge Graduate Institute. February 29, 2008.

Chapter 5: Interview with Bruce Herbert, Principal—Newground Social Investment. February 20, 2008.

Chapter 6: Interview with Maria Damon, Professor of Economics— University of Washington. February 7, 2008.

Chapter 7: Interview with Rhys Roth, Co-Director—Climate Solutions. February 6, 2008.

Chapter 9: Interview with Michelle Rupp, CEO—NRG Seattle. February 7, 2008.

Chapter 11: Interview with Marty McDonald, Principal—Egg. February 29, 2008.

Chapter 11: Interview with Bert Gregory, CEO—Mithun. March 18, 2008.

Chapter 13: Interview with Wood Turner, Executive Director—Climate Counts. February 11, 2008.

TEXT BOX REFERENCES

Chapter 2

[a.] Interview with Kevin Hagen, CSR Manager, REI. February 11, 2008.

Chapter 3

[b.] Interview with Steve Leahy, President, Greater Seattle Chamber of Commerce. February 21, 2008.
[c.] Albion, Mark. *Making a Life, Making a Living: Reclaiming Your Purpose and Passion in Business and in Life.* Warner Books, 2000

Chapter 4

[d.] Interview with Gifford Pinchot, President—Bainbridge Graduate Institute. February 29, 2008.

Chapter 5

[e.] Ruckelshaus, William. "Toward A Sustainable World." *The Energy-Environment Connection.* Ed. Jack Hollander. Island Press, 1992. 373.
[f.] "Reducing U.S. Greenhouse Gas Emissions: How Much at What Cost?" Dec 2007. McKinsey & Company. 12 Oct 2008 http://www.mckinsey.com/clientservice/ccsi/greenhousegas.asp

Chapter 6

[g.] Interview with Maria Damon, Professor of Economics—University of Washington. February 7, 2008.

Chapter 7

[h.] Alsop, Phil. "EMC introduces new services and tools for optimising energy efficiency in the data centre". 07 Dec 2006. DataCenter Solutions. 08 Jun 2008 http://www.datacentresols.com/news/articles-full.php?newsid=5316

[i.] Interview with Rhys Roth, Co-Director—Climate Solutions. February 6, 2008.

Chapter 9

[j.] Interview with Michelle Rupp, CEO—NRG Seattle. February 7, 2008.

Chapter 10

[k.] "Wal-Mart Expands Leadership On Energy Efficiency, Ethical Sourcing And Health Care". 23 Jan 2008. Wal-Mart, Inc. 08 Aug 2008 http://walmartstores.com/FactsNews/NewsRoom/7894.aspx

[l.] Business for Social Responsibility | Perspectives on Information Management in Sustainable Supply Chains | August 2007

Chapter 11

[m.] Interview with Marty McDonald, Principal—Egg. February 29, 2008.

[n.] Laczniak and Murphy. "Normative Perspectives for Ethical and Socially Responsible Marketing". *Journal of Macromarketing.* 26 (2006):154.

[o.] Willard, Bob. "The Next Sustainability Wave". New Society Publishers, 2005. 267

Chapter 12

[p.] Interview with Wood Turner, Executive Director—Climate Counts. February 11, 2008.

ENDNOTES

FOREWORD AND INTRODUCTION

[i] "IPPC Fourth Assessment Report: Climate Change 2007." Intergovernmental Panel on Climate Change. 10 Jan. 2008 <http://www.ipcc.ch/ipccreports/assessments-reports.htm>.

[ii] Reid, Walter V., et al. Millennium Ecosystem Assessment: Ecosystems and Human Well-being: Synthesis. Washington, DC. Island Press, 2005.

[iii] "World Footprint: Do we fit on the planet?" 2008. Global Footprint Network. 10 Dec. 2008 <http://www.footprintnetwork.org/en/index.php/GFN/page/world_footprint/>.

[iv] "Global Environment Outlook: Environment for Development (GEO-4)." 25 Oct. 2007. United Nations Environment Programme (UNEP). 10 Jan. 2008 <http://www.unep.org/geo/geo4/media/>.

[v] "United Nations Decade of Education for Sustainable Development." 2008. UNESCO. 10 Jan. 2008 <http://portal.unesco.org/education/en/ev.php-URL_ID=27234&URL_DO=DO_TOPIC&URL_SECTION=201.html>.

[vi] "Genuine Progress Indicator." 2008. Redefining Progress. 10 Jan. 2008 <http://www.rprogress.org/sustainability_indicators/genuine_progress_indicator.htm>.

[vii] Dauncey, Guy, and P. Mazza. Stormy Weather: 101 Solutions to Global Climate Change. Gabriola Island, BC. Canada. New Society Publishers, 2001.

[viii] "IPPC Fourth Assessment Report: Climate Change 2007." Intergovernmental Panel on Climate Change. 10 Jan. 2008 <http://www.ipcc.ch/ipccreports/assessments-reports.htm>.

CHAPTER 1: THE CLIMATE IMPERATIVE

[ix] Choi, Charles Q. "Warming May Make 'Perfect Storm' of Disease." 24 June 2008. *LiveScience*. 14 June 2008 <http://www.livescience.com/health/080624-storm-plague.html>.

[x] Intergovernmental Panel on Climate Change. *Temperature Change (1760–2100)*. 14 June 2008 <http://www.ipcc.ch/graphics/graphics/2001wg1/small/05.02.jpg>.

[xi] Deyo, Holly. *Natural Disasters Reported, 1900–2007*. 24 June 2008 <http://standeyo.com/News_Files/UN_Images/nat.disasters.1900-2007.jpg>.

[xii] "Working Group 1 Report: The Physical Science Basis." Aug. 2008. *IPCC Fourth Assessment Report* 2007. Intergovernmental Panel on Climate Change. 10 Jan. 2008 <http://www.ipcc.ch/ipccreports/ar4-wg1.htm>.

[xiii] Velazquez, Jerry. "Disaster Risk Reduction and Climate Change Adaptation— Avoiding the Unmanageable, Managing the Unavoidable." 18 June 2008.The World Bank. 24 June 2008 <http://siteresources.worldbank.org/PHILIPPINESEXTN/Resources/01_ISDRArticle_Climat.pdf>.

[xiv] LaMonica, Martin. "Is it time to talk about 'peak water'?" 29 April 2008. *CNET News*. 24 June 2008 <http://news.cnet.com/8301-11128_3-9931294-54.html>.

[xv] "Insights from the Comprehensive Assessment of Water Management in Agriculture." Aug. 2006. International Water Management Institute. 24 June 2008 <http://news.bbc.co.uk/2/shared/bsp/hi/pdfs/21_08_06_world_water_week.pdf>.

[xvi] "Deserts, Drylands and Desertification Through the Eyes of Children." 23 Sep. 2005. United Nations Environment Programme. 14 June 2008 <http://www.unep.org/Documents.Multilingual/Default.asp?DocumentID=452&ArticleID=4959&l=en>.

[xvii] "350 : Global Warming. Global Action. Global Future. " 2008. 7 July 2008 <http://www.350.org>.

[xviii] "How to Cut Global Warming Emissions in Half." Recreated by K. Wilhelm 08 June 2008 with permission from NRDC. 08 June 2008 <www.nrdc.org/air/energy/rep/images/figu1.gif>.

CHAPTER 2: CARBON FOOTPRINTING

[xix] Putt del Pino, Samantha, et al. "Hot Climate, Cool Commerce: A Service Sector Guide to Greenhouse Gas Management." May 2006. World Resource Institute. 7 July 2008 <http://pdf.wri.org/hotclimatecoolcommerce.pdf>.

[xx] Putt del Pino, Samantha, et al. "Hot Climate, Cool Commerce: A Service Sector Guide to Greenhouse Gas Management." May 2006. World Resource Institute. 7 July 2008 <http://pdf.wri.org/hotclimatecoolcommerce.pdf>.

[xxi] "ISO, WRI and WBCSD Announce Cooperation on Greenhouse Gas Accounting and Verification." 3 Dec. 2007. World Resources Institute. 4 Aug. 2008 <http://www.wri.org/press/2007/12/iso-wri-and-wbcsd-announce-cooperation-greenhouse-gas-accounting-and-verification#>.

CHAPTER 3: BUSINESS BENEFIT

[xxii] "Open Work Is for Everyone." 22 Dec. 2008. Sun Microsystems. 4 Aug. 2008 <http://www.sun.com/service/openwork/success.html>.

[xxiii] Clark, Tim. "10 Trends and Technologies Driving Secure Telecommuting." Sep. 2008. The FactPoint Group. 24 Sep. 2008 <http://www.sun.com/aboutsun/csr/report2007/eco/carbon_greening.jsp>

[xxiv] "Planet Payback: Reduce What We Can. Offset What We Can't." Dec. 2008. Yakima. 24 Sep. 2008 <www.yakimapayback.com>.

[xxv] Beckley, Bill. Personal interview. 4 Aug. 2008.

[xxvi] Hoffman, Andrew. "Getting Ahead of the Curve: Corporate Strategies That Address Climate Change." 7 June 2007. Pew Center on Global Climate Change. 24 Sep. 2008 <http://www.pewclimate.org/docUploads/DuPoint%20case%20study.pdf>.

[xxvii] Romm, Joseph, and W. Browning. *Greening and the Bottom Line: Increasing Productivity Through Energy-Efficient Design.* Boulder, CO. Rocky Mountain Inst, Dec. 1994.

[xxviii] "Lockheed Expands into Energy Conservation Market." 22 Jan. 2008. World Business Council for Sustainable Development. 4 April 2008 <http://www.wbcsd.org/plugins/DocSearch/details.asp?type=DocDet&ObjectId=MjgxNzg>.

[xxix] Pierson, Randi. Personal interview. 30 June 2008.

[xxx] "Success Story: River Run Bed and Breakfast." April 2008. ENERGY STAR. 8 April 2008
<http://www.energystar.gov/index.cfm?c=sb_success.sb_successstories_riverrun>
.
[xxxi] "Success Story: Columbus Hospitality Group." April 2008. ENERGY STAR 8 April 2008
<http://www.energystar.gov/index.cfm?c=hospitality.bus_hospitality_columbus>.
[xxxii] "Proud to be Green." Dec. 2008. Association of Bay Area Governments. 14 Dec. 2008
<http://www.abag.ca.gov/bayarea/bayarea_info/enviro/gbus/proud.html>.
[xxxiii] "Commitment to Sustainability." Dec. 2008. Wendel Rosen Black & Dean LLP. 14 Dec. 2008 <http://www.wendel.com/firm_overview.cfm>.
[xxxiv] "Proud to Be Green." Dec. 2008. Association of Bay Area Governments. 14 Dec. 2008
<http://www.abag.ca.gov/bayarea/bayarea_info/enviro/gbus/proud.html>.
[xxxv] "Innovation Wednesday: Wal-Mart Surpasses Goal to Sell 100 Million Compact Fluorescents Three Months Early: CEO H. Lee Scott Celebrates with Some Hamburger Helper." 3 Oct. 2007. Fast Company. 6 June 2008
<http://blog.fastcompany.com/archives/2007/10/03/innovation_wednesday_walm art_surpasses_goal_to_sell_100_million_compact_fluorescent_light_bulbs_three_ months_early_ceo_h_lee_scott_celebrates_with_some_hamburger_helper.html>.
[xxxvi] Crown, Judith. "Food: Always Room for Profits." BusinessWeek. (21 Feb. 2008). 6 June 2008
<http://www.businessweek.com/bwdaily/dnflash/content/feb2008/db20080220_00 9749.htm?chan=top+news_top+news+index_businessweek+exclusives>.
[xxxvii] "50 Ways to Green Your Business." Nov. 2007. Fast Company. 6 June 2008
<http://www.fastcompany.com/magazine/120/50-ways-to-green-your-business.html>.
[xxxviii] "Success Stories: Telecommunications." 6 June 2008. WasteWise, a program of the US EPA. 6 June 2008
<http://epa.gov/epawaste/partnerships/wastewise/success/telecom.htm>.
[xxxix] Kroman, John (Partner, Garvey Schubert Barer). Personal interview. 11 Feb 2008.
[xl] Burroughs, Kim. Personal interview. 12 Feb 2008.

CHAPTER 4: RETURN ON SUSTAINABILITY (ROS)

[xli] "The Business Case." 3 Oct. 2008. Burgerville. 3 Oct. 2008 <http://www.burgerville.com/#page:/Sustainable-Business/The-Business-Case.aspx|secNum:4|subSecNum:2>.
[xlii] Elkington, John. Cannibals with Forks: The Triple Bottom Line of 21st Century Business. Oxford: Capstone Publishing, 1997.
[xliii] "Compact Fluorescent Light bulbs." Dec. 2008. ENERGY STAR. 9 Aug. 2008 <http://www.energystar.gov/index.cfm?c=cfls.pr_cfls>.

CHAPTER 5: PUBLIC POLICY

[xliv] The Intergovernmental Panel on Climate Change. 12 Aug. 2008 <http://www.ipcc.ch/>.
[xlv] "What's Being Done…In the States." Dec. 2008. The Pew Center on Global Climate Change. 12 Aug. 2008 <http://www.pewclimate.org/what_s_being_done/in_the_states/>.
[xlvi] "What's Being Done…In the States." Dec. 2008. The Pew Center on Global Climate Change. 12 Aug. 2008 <http://www.pewclimate.org/what_s_being_done/in_the_states/>.
[xlvii] "Cities That Have Signed On." Dec. 2008. Mayors Climate Protection Center. 22 Dec. 2008 <http://www.usmayors.org/climateprotection /ClimateChange.asp>.
[xlviii] Vogel, David. "Socially Responsible Lobbying." Harvard Business Review. Feb 2008: 41.
[xlix] "Cities That Have Signed On." Dec. 2008. Mayors Climate Protection Center. 22 Dec. 2008 <http://www.usmayors.org/climateprotection/ClimateChange.asp>.
[l] "State Legislation from Around the Country." Dec. 2008. Pew Center on Global Climate Change. 22 Sep. 2008 <http://www.pewclimate.org/what_s_being_done/in_the_states/state_legislation.cfm>.
[li] "Climate Change Initiatives and Programs in the States." Dec. 2008. Pew Center on Global Climate Change. 22 Sep. 2008 <http://www.pewclimate.org/docUploads/States%20table%203%2027%2008.pdf>.
[lii] "What's Being Done…In the States." Dec. 2008. The Pew Center on Global Climate Change. 12 Aug. 2008 <http://www.pewclimate.org/what_s_being_done/in_the_states/>.

liii "State Climate Actions." Dec. 2008. US Environmental Protection Agency. 22 Sep. 2008 <http://epa.gov/climatechange/wycd/stateandlocalgov/state.html>.

liv "Vehicle Greenhouse Gas Emissions Standards." Dec. 2008. Pew Center on Global Climate Change. 22 Sep. 2008 <http://www.pewclimate.org/what_s_being_done/in_the_states/vehicle_ ghg_standard.cfm>.

lv "Vehicle Greenhouse Gas Emissions Standards." Dec. 2008. Pew Center on Global Climate Change. 22 Sep. 2008 <http://www.pewclimate.org/what_s_being_done/in_the_states/vehicle_ ghg_standard.cfm>.

lvi "States with Renewable Portfolio Standards." Dec. 2008. US Department of Energy Efficiency and Renewable Energy. 22 Sep. 2008 <http://www.eere.energy.gov/states/maps/renewable_portfolio_states.cfm #chart>.

lvii Attinger, Steve. "Extended Producer Responsibility: Making Green from Green." 10 Nov. 2006. Greenbiz.com. 12 Sep. 2008 <http://www.greenbiz.com/news/news_third.cfm?NewsID=34241&CFID=909203&CFTOKEN=21670746>.

lviii "Top 10 Industries with Largest Total On-Site and Off-Site Disposal and Other Releases, 2002." 22 June 2004. US Environmental Protection Agency. 22 Sep. 2008 <http://www.epa.gov/tri/tridata/tri02/pdr/Rel-10indus-2002.pdf>.

lix "Commercial Building Energy Codes." Dec. 2008. Pew Center on Global Climate Change. 22 Sep. 2008 <http://www.pewclimate.org/what_s_being_done/in_the_states/comm__ energy_codes.cfm>.

lx "What is REACH?" Dec. 2008. EUROPA: Gateway to the European Union. 22 Sept 2008 <http://ec.europa.eu/environment/chemicals/reach/reach_intro.htm>.

CHAPTER 6: CARBON TAXES & CAP AND TRADE

lxi "City Residents Vote to Tax Selves for Carbon Use." 10 Nov. 2006. MSNBC. 7 June 2008 <http://www.msnbc.msn.com/id/15651688/>.

lxii Chan, Sewell. "Bloomberg Calls for Tax on Carbon Emissions." 2 Nov. 2007. 7 June 2008 <http://cityroom.blogs.nytimes.com/2007/11/02/bloomberg-calls-for-tax-on-carbon-emissions/>.

lxiii "Policy Options for Reducing Greenhouse Gas Emissions." Feb. 2008. Congressional Budget Office. 7 June 2008 <http://www.cbo.gov/ftpdocs/89xx/doc8934/02-12-Carbon.pdf>.

lxiv Brouillard, Carolyn, and S. Van Pelt. "A Community Takes Charge: Boulder's Carbon Tax." Feb. 2007. City of Boulder, Colorado. 9 June 2008

<http://www.bouldercolorado.gov/files/Environmental%20Affairs/climate%20and%20energy/boulders_carbon_tax.pdf>.

lxv Brouillard, Carolyn, and S. Van Pelt. "A Community Takes Charge: Boulder's Carbon Tax." Feb. 2007. City of Boulder, Colorado. 9 June 2008 <http://www.bouldercolorado.gov/files/Environmental%20Affairs/climate%20and%20energy/boulders_carbon_tax.pdf>.

lxvi "City Residents Vote to Tax Selves for Carbon Use." 10 Nov. 2006. MSNBC. 7 June 2008 <http://www.msnbc.msn.com/id/15651688/>.

lxvii "The Carbon Tax: The Pros and Cons of a Tax on Fossil Fuel." 16 June 2006. CBC News. 9 June 2008 <http://www.cbc.ca/news /background/kyoto/carbon-tax.html>.

lxviii Dougherty, Kevin. "Quebec to Bring in Canada's First Carbon Tax on Fuel." 7 June 2007. CanWest News Service. 9 June 2008 <http://www.canada.com/topics/news/politics/story.html?id=ef788840-ec3f-4536-8253-7c35660cc4aa&k=70073>.

lxix Dougherty, Kevin. "Quebec to Bring in Canada's First Carbon Tax on Fuel." 7 June 2007. CanWest News Service. 9 June 2008 <http://www.canada.com/topics/news/politics/story.html?id=ef788840-ec3f-4536-8253-7c35660cc4aa&k=70073>.

lxx "BC's Revenue Neutral Carbon Tax." Feb. 2008. Province of British Columbia. 9 June 2008 <http://www.bcbudget.gov.bc.ca/2008/backgrounders /backgrounder_carbon_tax.htm>.

lxxi "B.C. Carbon Tax Kicks in on Canada Day." July 2008. CBC News. 7 June 2008 <http://www.cbc.ca/canada/british-columbia/story/2008/06/30/bc-carbon-tax-effective.html?ref=rss>.

lxxii Meissner, Dirk. "BC Introduces Carbon Tax, but Off-Sets Increased Fuel Costs with Tax Cuts." 20 Feb. 2008. The Canadian Press. 9 June 2008 <http://www.princegeorgecitizen.com/20080219119025/wire/national-news/bc-introduces-carbon-tax-but-off-sets-increased-fuel-costs-with-tax-cuts.html>.

lxxiii "Cap and Trade: Essentials." US Environmental Protection Agency. 10 June 2008 <http://www.epa.gov/airmarkets/cap-trade/docs/ctessentials.pdf>.

lxxiv "The Cap and Trade Success Story." Feb. 2007. Environmental Defense Fund. 8 June 2008 <http://www.edf.org/page.cfm?tagID=1085>.

lxxv "The Cap and Trade Success Story." Feb. 2007. Environmental Defense Fund. 8 Jun 2008 <http://www.edf.org/page.cfm?tagID=1085>.

[lxxvi] Coile, Zachary, et al. "EPA Blocks California Bid to Limit Greenhouse Gases from Cars." 20 Dec. 2007. *San Francisco Chronicle*. 8 June 2008 <http://www.sfgate.com/c/a/2007/12/02/MNMMTJUS1.DTL>.

[lxxvii] "Cap and Trade: Essentials." US Environmental Protection Agency. 10 June 2008 <http://www.epa.gov/airmarkets/cap-trade/docs/ctessentials.pdf>.

lxxviii European Climate Exchange. 9 June 2008 <http://www.europeanclim ateexchange.com/default_flash.asp>.

[lxxix] Johnson, Toni. "The Debate over Greenhouse Gas Cap-and-Trade." 20 Sep. 2007. Council on Foreign Relations. 9 June 2008 <http://www.cfr.org/publication /14231/debate_over_greenhouse_gas_ capandtrade.html>.

[lxxx] "CDM Statistics." Dec. 2008. United Nations Framework Convention on Climate Change. 22 Dec. 2008 <http://cdm.unfccc.int/Statistics/index.html>.

[lxxxi] "CDM CERs Distribution by Country." Feb. 2007. *Wikimedia*. 6 June 2008 <http://commons.wikimedia.org/wiki/File:CDM_CERs_distribution_by_country.p ng>.

[lxxxii] "Payments for Ecosystem Services: Market Profiles." May 2008. The Ecosystem Marketplace. 12 June 2008 <http://ecosystemmarketplace.com /documents/acrobat/PES_Matrix_Profiles_PROFOR.pdf>.

[lxxxii] Mortished, Carl. "Shell Chief Fears Oil Shortage in Seven Years." 25 Jan. 2008. *The Times Online*. 9 June 2008 <http://business.timesonline.co.uk/tol /business/economics/wef/article3248484.ece>.

[lxxxiii] "Annual Energy Outlook 2008 with Projections to 2030." 8 Aug. 2008. US Department of Energy's Energy Information Association. 16 Aug. 2008 <http://www.eia.doe.gov/oiaf/aeo/pdf/0383(2008).pdf>.

[lxxxiv] "Oil Posts Biggest-Ever 1-Day Gain: Futures Finish up $16.37—After Being up More than $25 to $130—on the Bailout Plan, the Falling Dollar and the Expiration of the October Contract." 22 Sep. 2008. CNN Money. 22 Sep. 2008 <http://money.cnn.com/2008/09/22/markets/oil/index.htm>.

[lxxxv] "Oil to Stay over $100 Through 2009: EIA." 2 June 2008. Reuters. 2 June 2008 <http://www.reuters.com/article/idUSN0229036420080603>.

CHAPTER 7: ENERGY

[lxxxvii] "Peak Oil Primer." June 2008. Energy Bulletin. 8 June 2008 <www.energybulletin.net/primer.php>.

[lxxxviii] "The Growing Gap: Oil Discovery and Production." 2002. The Association for the Study of Peak Oil. 9 June 2008 <http://www.peakoil.net/>.

[lxxxix] Doran, James. "Fuel Costs Kill off a US Airline Every Week." May 2008. *The Observer.* 9 June 2008 <http://www.guardian.co.uk/business/2008 /may/25/theairlineindustry.usa>.

[xc] Curry, Tim. "Governing the United States of Coal. Urgent Problem for Coal-State Governors: Power Plants' Carbon Dioxide." 25 Feb. 2008. MSNBC. 14 June 2008 <http://www.msnbc.msn.com/id/23322827/>.

[xci] "The Fifth Power and Conservation Plan." May 2005. Northwest Power and Conservation Council. 12 June 2008 <http://www.nwcouncil.org/ energy/powerplan/5/Default.htm>.

[xcii] "Fred Hutchinson Cancer Research Center Wins Three Environmental Awards Including the Top Award, the Mayor's Environmental Leadership Award." May 2004. Fred Hutchinson Cancer Research Center. 12 June 2008 <http://www.fhcrc.org/about/ne/news/2004/05/19/environmental.html>.

[xciii] "Fred Hutchinson Cancer Research Center Wins Three Environmental Awards Including the Top Award, the Mayor's Environmental Leadership Award." May 2004. Fred Hutchinson Cancer Research Center. 12 June 2008 <http://www.fhcrc.org/about/ne/news/2004/05/19/environmental.html>.

[xciv] "High Performance Buildings Deliver Increased Retail Sales." July 2000. City of Seattle. 6 June 2008 <http://www.seattle.gov/light/conserve /sustainability/studies/cv5_ss.htm>.

[xcv] "Carbon down Profits up, Third Edition." Feb. 2007. The Climate Group. 14 June 2008 <http://www.theclimategroup.org/assets/resources/cdpu_ newedition.pdf>.

[xcvi] Interview with Kevin Hagen. 11 Feb 2008.

[xcvii] "About Us." June 2008. World Resources Institute. 16 June 2008 <http://www.thegreenpowergroup.org/aboutus.cfm?loc=us>.

[xcviii] "Intel Becomes Largest Purchaser of Green Power in the U.S." Jan .2008. Intel. 8 June 2008 <http://www.intel.com/pressroom/archive/releases/20080128 corp.htm>.

[xcix] "Pepsi Tops List of Green Power Purchasers." July 2007. Environmental Leader. 17 June 2008 <http://www.environmentalleader.com/2007/07/31/pepsi-tops-list-of-green-power-purchasers/>.

ᶜ "Green Pricing." June 2008. US Department of Energy Efficiency and Renewable Energy. 6 June 2008 <http://www.eere.energy.gov /greenpower/markets/pricing.shtml?page=2& companyid=39>.

CHAPTER 8: FINANCE

ᶜⁱ McCarthy, Bill."Banks Strict with Clean-Coal Lending." 8 Feb. 2008. *Wyoming Tribune-Eagle Online.* 17 June 2008 http://www.wyomingnews.com/articles/2008/02/08/local_news_updates/19local_ 02-08-08.prt.

ᶜⁱⁱ *The Equator Principles.* 17 June 2008 <http://www.equator-principles.com/index.shtml>.

ᶜⁱⁱⁱ "Preamble." July 2008. *The Equator Principles.* 17 July 2008 <http://www.equator-principles.com/principles.shtml>.

ᶜⁱᵛ "Consultiva Internacional, Inc." 2005. 10 July 2008 <www.consultiva.com/data/PRI_english.doc>.

ᶜᵛ "Banks, Businesses Seek Answers on Climate Change." 4 July 2008. Environmental Finance. 10 July 2008 <http://www.environmental-finance.com/onlinews/0111ban.htm>.

ᶜᵛⁱ "Banks, Businesses Seek Answers on Climate Change." 4 July 2008. Environmental Finance. 10 July 2008 <http://www.environmental-finance.com/onlinews/0111ban.htm>.

ᶜᵛⁱⁱ "London Accord Maps out How $600 Billion a Year Investment Market Can Be Shifted to Help Roll Back Climate Change." 3 Dec. 2007. City of London. 10 July 2008 <http://www.corpoflondon.gov.uk/Corporation/media_centre/files2007/ london_accord_maps_out.htm>.

ᶜᵛⁱⁱⁱ "The Environment." July 2008. Citigroup. 10 July 2008 <http://www.citigroup.com/citigroup/environment/climatechange.htm>.

ᶜⁱˣ Wilson, David. "Foreclosures May Blunt Treasury Aid, Whitney Says: Chart of Day." 15 Oct. 2008. Bloomberg. 18 Oct 2008 http://www.bloomberg.com/apps/news?pid=20601109&sid=a01xg_Vb5mf8&refe r=patrick.net.

ᶜˣ "The Buck Stops Here: How Securitization Changed the Rules for Ordinary Americans." 10 Sep. 2008. Interfaith Center on Corporate Responsibility (ICCR).

10 Sep. 2008 <http://www.iccr.org/news/press_releases/2008/pr_subprime
091008.htm>.

[cxi] "The Buck Stops Here: How Securitization Changed the Rules for Ordinary
Americans." 10 Sep. 2008. Interfaith Center on Corporate Responsibility (ICCR).
10 Sep. 2008 <http://www.iccr.org/news/press_releases/2008/pr_subprime
091008.htm>.

[cxii] "Socially Responsible Investing in the US and Europe: Same Goals but
Different Paths." March 2007. Celent. 10 July 2008
<http://www.celent.com/PressReleases/20070313/SRI.htm>.

[cxiii] "2007 Report on Socially Responsible Investing Trends in the United States."
Jan. 2008. Social Investment Forum. 10 July 2008
<http://www.socialinvest.org/pdf/SRI_Trends_ExecSummary_2007.pdf>.

[cxiv] Liptow, Jennifer. "Warming up to SRI." March 2007. Financial Planning. 10
July 2008 <http://www.financial-planning.com/asset/article/528056/channel
/231/warming-up-sri.html?pg=>.

[cxv] "Socially Responsible Investing in the US and Europe: Same Goals but
Different Paths." March 2007. Celent. 10 July 2008 <http://www.celent.com
/PressReleases/20070313/SRI.htm>.

[cxvi] "AIM Environmental Technology Program." March 2008. CalPERS. 10 July
2008 <http://www.calpers.ca.gov/index.jsp?bc=/investments/environ-invest/aim-
environ-tech-prog/home.xml>.

[cxvii] "Environmental Investment Initiatives." March 2008. CalPERS. 10 July 2008
<http://www.calpers.ca.gov/index.jsp?bc=/investments/environ-invest/home.xml>.

[cxviii] "Environmental Investment Initiatives." March 2008. CalPERS. 10 July 2008
<http://www.calpers.ca.gov/index.jsp?bc=/investments/environ-invest/home.xml>.

[cxix] "CalPERS Puts $2B into Sustainable Forestry." 19 Feb. 2008. *Sacramento
Business Journal.* 10 July 2008 <http://www.bizjournals.com/sacramento/stories
/2008/02/18/daily20.html>.

[cxx] "Investors Achieve Major Company Commitments on Climate Change." 20
Aug. 2008. Ceres. 24 Aug. 2008 <http://www.ceres.org/NETCOMMUNITY
/Page.aspx?pid=227&srcid =601>.

[cxxi] Donnelly, John. "U.S. Institutional Investors Sign Pact Urging Congress to
Enact 'Green' Legislation." 20 March 2007. *The Boston Globe.* 10 July 2008
<http://www.iht.com/articles/2007/03/20/business/warm.php>.

[cxxii] "Facts at a Glance: General." Oct. 2008. CalPERS. 10 Nov. 2008
<http://www.calpers.ca.gov/eip-docs/about/facts/general.pdf>.

cxxiii "Calvert Social Investment Fund Balanced Portfolio (CSIFX)." July 2008. *Calvert Online*. 10 July 2008 <http://www.calvertgroup.com/funds_profile.html ?fund=905&keepleftnav=Fund%20Information>.

cxxiv Dow Jones Sustainability Index. 10 July 2008 <http://www.sustainability-indexes.com/07_htmle/indexes/overview.html>.

cxxv Jantzi Social Index. 13 Feb. 2008 <http://www.jantzi socialindex.com/index.asp?section=9&level_2=0&level_3=0&pr_id=146>.

cxxvi Carbon Disclosure Project. 16 July 2008 <http://www.cdproject.net/>.

cxxvii "Introducing GS SUSTAIN." 22 June 2007. Goldman Sachs. 10 July 2008 <http://www.unglobalcompact.org/docs/summit2007/gs_esg_embargoed_until030 707pdf.pdf>.

cxxviii "Clean technology" is a broad term for sustainability technology; it encompasses such industries such as biofuels, solar energy, wind energy, vehicle electrification, green building, and biological sequestration.

cxxix "Cleantech Venture Capital: How Public Policy Has Stimulated Private Investment." May 2007. Environmental Entrepreneurs. 10 July 2008 <http://www.e2.org/ext/doc/CleantechReport2007.pdf;jsessionid=D66FC813593B C02BAB9D80B1C564A253>.

cxxx Green VC. "Global Cleantech VC Investment Reached $3 Billion in 2007." 3 March 2008. 18 July 2008 <http://www.greenvc.org/2008/03/cleantech-vc-in.html>.

cxxxi Mendell, Emily, et al. "Cleantech Venture Investments by US Firms Break Record in 2007." Nov. 2007. National Venture Capital Association. 18 July 2008 <http://www.nvca.org/pdf/CleanTechInterimPR.pdf>.

cxxxii "Money Tree Report." July 2008. PriceWaterhouseCoopers. 18 July 2008 <https://www.pwcmoneytree.com/MTPublic/ns/index.jsp>.

cxxxiii "Global BioFuels Market Exceeds Wind and Solar as Clean Energy Revenues Soar to $40 Billion in 2005, Reports Clean Edge; U.S. Venture Capital Investments Reach $917 Million in 2005, up 28 Percent from 2004." March 2006. Business Wire. 18 July 2008 <http://www.businesswire.com/portal/site/google /?ndmViewId=news_view&newsId=20060307005034&newsLang=en>.

cxxxiv Mitchell, Russ. "Behind the Green Doerr." May 2007. *Portfolio.com*. 18 July 2008 <http://www.portfolio.com/executives/features/2007/03/29/Behind-the-Green-Doerr>.

cxxxiv Krupp, Fred. "The Mother Lode." April 2008. Fast Company. 2 June 2008. <http://www.fastcompany.com/magazine/124/the-mother-lode.html>.

CHAPTER 9: INSURANCE

cxxxv "Betting on a Green Future." April 2006. Wired. 12 July 2008 <http://www.wired.com/science /discoveries/news/2006/04/70641>.

cxxxvi Heilprin, John. "Gore Warns on Subprime Carbon Industry." Feb. 2008. Associated Press. 12 July 2008 <http://www.thefreelibrary.com/Gore+warns+on+'subprime+carbon'+industry-a01610906388>.

cxxxvii "Our Position and Objectives." July 2008. Swiss Re. 18 July 2008 <http://www.swissre.com/pws/about%20us/knowledge_expertise/top%20topics/our%20position%20and%20objectives.html?contentIDR=c21767004561734fb900fb2ee2bd2155&useDefaultText=0&useDefaultDesc=0>.

cxxxviii Wolk, Martin. "How Hurricane Katrina's Costs Are Adding up." 13 Sep. 2005. MSNBC. 12 July 2008 <http://www.msnbc.msn.com/id/9329293/>.

cxxxix "Hurricane Rita: The Impact." Sep. 2005. BBC News. 18 July 2008 <http://news.bbc.co.uk/2/hi/americas/4276284.stm>.

cxl "Climate Change: Financial Risks to Federal and Private Insurers in Coming Decades are Potentially Significant." April 2007. The Government Accountability Office. 15 July 2008 http://www.gao.gov/new.items/d07760t.pdf.

cxli McQueen, MP. "Hurricane Watch: Insurers Criticized for New Rate Models." The Wall Street Journal 1 July 2008: A1.

cxlii "Climate Change: Financial Risks to Federal and Private Insurers in Coming Decades are Potentially Significant." April 2007. The Government Accountability Office. 15 July 2008 <http://www.gao.gov/new.items/d07760t.pdf>.

cxliii "Climate Change: Financial Risks to Federal and Private Insurers in Coming Decades are Potentially Significant." April 2007. The Government Accountability Office. 15 July 2008 <http://www.gao.gov/new.items/d07760t.pdf>.

cxliv "Tackling Climate Change." May 2008. Swiss Re. 1 Aug. 2008 <http://www.swissre.com/pws/research%20publications/top%20topics%20view/tackling%20climate%20change.html>.

cxlv "Climate Change and Global Warming (EX) Task Force." Aug. 2008. National Association of Insurance Commissioners. 11 Aug. 2008 <http://www.naic.org/committees_ex_climate.htm>.

cxlvi climateandinsurance.org. 2008. Climate and Insurance. 08 Aug 2008

cxlvii "About Disaster Safety." Institute for Business & Home Safety. 8 Aug. 2008. <http://www.disastersafety.org/about/>.

[cxlviii] "Environment. " Aug. 2008. Allstate. 10 Aug. 2008 <http://www.allstate.com/citizenship/environment/environmental-respon sibility.aspx>.

[cxlix] "Climate Change." Dec. 2008. State Farm Insurance. 12 Aug. 2008 <http://www.statefarm.com/about/media/current/climate.asp>.

[cl] "Exclusive: Whistleblowers Say State Farm Cheated Katrina Victims." Aug. 2006. ABC News. 11 Aug. 2008 <http://blogs.abcnews.com/theblotter/2006 /08/state_farm_insi.html>.

[cli] "Trent Lott Sues State Farm over Katrina Damage." Dec. 2005. Consumer Affairs. 11 Aug. 2008 <http://www.consumeraffairs.com/news04/2005/ katrina_lott.html>.

[clii] "What We Do." 2008. Esurance. 9 Aug. 2008 <http://www. esurance.com/home/whatwedo.asp>.

[cliii] "Business and Climate Reports." Aug. 2008. Ceres. 11 Aug. 2008 <http://www.pewclimate.org/business/external-reports>.

[cliv] "Business and Climate Reports." Aug. 2008. Ceres. 11 Aug. 2008 <http://www.pewclimate.org/business/external-reports>.

[clv] Andel, Tom. "Make Your Supply Chain Sustainable." July 2007. Material Handling Industry of America. 13 Dec. 2007 <http://www. mhia.org/articles/7_16_07.cfm>.

[clvi] "Wal Mart Pledges Packaging Reduction." Dec. 2008. Wal Mart. 1 Sep. 2008 <http://walmartstores.com/Sustainability/7983.aspx>.

[clvii] "The Lean and Green Supply Chain: A Practical Guide for Materials Managers and Supply Chain Managers to Reduce Costs and Improve Environmental Performance." Jan. 2007. US Environmental Protection Agency. 12 June 2008 <http://www.epa.gov/oppt/library/pubs/archive/acct-archive/pubs /lean.pdf>.

[clviii] "Wal-Mart Launches 5-Year Plan to Reduce Packaging." Sep. 2006. Wal Mart. 12 Sep. 2008 <http://walmartstores.com/FactsNews/NewsRoom/5951.aspx>.

[clix] "HP, L'Oreal, Pepsi, Others Asking Suppliers for Emissions Info." Jan. 2008. Environmental Leader. 12 Sep. 2008 <http://www. environmentalleader.com/2008/01/21/hp-loreal-pepsi-others-asking-suppliers-for-emissions-info/>.

[clx] Herrera, Tilde. "Dole's Quest for a Carbon Neutral Supply Chain." Nov. 2007. Kiplinger Business Resource Center. 2 Sep. 2008 <http://www.

kiplinger.com/businessresource/summary/archive/2007/greentips_carbonneutral.ht
ml>.

[clxi] Brun, Becky. "Surfers Stoked on Bio-Boards." March 2007. Sustainable
Industries Journal. 28 Aug. 2008 <http://www.sustainableindustries.
com/sijnews/6221836.html>.

[clxii] "Sears Pledges to Cut Use of PVC." 12 Dec. 2007. Yahoo! Finance. 28 Aug.
2008 <http://biz.yahoo.com/ap/071212/sears_pvc.html?.v=1>.

[clxiii] "Sears and Kmart Join Trend away from PVC Plastics." Dec. 2007.
Environment News Service. 28 Aug. 2008 <http://www.ens-
newswire.com/ens/dec2007/2007-12-14-091.asp>.

[clxiv] "Word Purchasing Policy." Sep. 2008. Home Depot. 22 Sep. 2008
<http://corporate.homedepot.com/wps/portal/Wood_Purchasing>.

[clxv] US Environmental Protection Agency. "The Lean and Green Supply Chain: A
Practical Guide for Materials Managers and Supply Chain Managers to Reduce
Costs and Improve Environmental Performance." Jan 2000:5.

[clxvi] "CSR Supply Chain Summit." 2008. China Supply Chain Council. 13 Dec.
2007 <http://www.supplychain.cn/en/cev/?292>.

[clxvii] "Nike, Inc.: A Natural Step Case Study." Jan. 2001. Oregon Natural Step. 2
Sep. 2008 <http://www.ortns.org/documents/ Nike.PDF>.

[clxviii] US Environmental Protection Agency. "The Lean and Green Supply Chain: A
Practical Guide for Materials Managers and Supply Chain Managers to Reduce
Costs and Improve Environmental Performance." Jan 2000: 4.

[clxix] Westervelt, Amy. "Biodegradable Packaging Market Expands." Sustainable
Industries Journal. Dec. 2007: 29.

[clxx] Westervelt, Amy. "Biodegradable Packaging Market Expands." Sustainable
Industries Journal. Dec. 2007: 29.

[clxxi] Penfield, Patrick. "The Green Supply Chain." Aug. 2007. Material Handling
Industry of America. 28 Aug. 2008 <http://www. mhia.org/articles/8_7_07.cfm>.

[clxxii] Penfield, Patrick. "The Green Supply Chain." Aug. 2007. Material Handling
Industry of America. 28 Aug. 2008 <http://www.mhia. org/articles/8_7_07.cfm>.

[clxxiii] "How SC Johnson Saved $1.6 Million with Efficient Trucking." Nov. 2007.
Environmental Leader. 28 Sep. 2008 <http://www.environmentalleader.
com/2007/11/29/how-sc-johnson-saved-16-million-with-efficient-trucking/>.

[clxxiv] Bigelow, Lauren. "Corporations Get Savvy with Cleantech." Sep. 2007.
Sustainable Industries. 28 Sep. 2008 <http://www.sustainableindustries.
com/commentary/10095541.html>.

clxxv "Wal-Mart Switches to Local Fruit, Veggies: Retail Giant Says It Is Now Biggest Buyer of Local Produce in U.S." Jul. 2008. CBS News. 2 Sep. 2008 <http://www.cbsnews.com/stories/2008/07/02/business/main4227280.shtml?sourc e=related_story>.

clxxvi US Environmental Protection Agency. "The Lean and Green Supply Chain: A Practical Guide for Materials Managers and Supply Chain Managers to Reduce Costs and Improve Environmental Performance." Jan 2000: 13.

clxxvii US Environmental Protection Agency. "The Lean and Green Supply Chain: A Practical Guide for Materials Managers and Supply Chain Managers to Reduce Costs and Improve Environmental Performance." Jan 2000: 13.

clxxviii US Environmental Protection Agency. "The Lean and Green Supply Chain: A Practical Guide for Materials Managers and Supply Chain Managers to Reduce Costs and Improve Environmental Performance." Jan 2000: 13.

clxxix Cole, Sam. "Zero Waste—On the Move Around the World." 2000. Eco-cycle. 28 Sep. 2008 <http://www.ecocycle.org/ZeroWaste/ZeroWasteon TheMove.cfm>.

clxxx Westervelt, Amy. "Toshiba Toes the Line on Take-Back." Sustainable Industries Journal. May 2007: 36

clxxxi "E-Waste Laws in Other States." Nov. 2008. Californians Against Waste. 12 Nov. 2008 <http://www.cawrecycles.org /issues/ca_e-waste/other_states>.

clxxxii Mahler, Daniel. "The Sustainable Supply Chain." Supply Chain Management Review. 11(8): 59.

CHAPTER 11: MARKETING TO GREEN CONSUMERS

clxxxiii "Serving the Climate-Change-Conscious Consumer: Summary Report Based on Consumer Research in the UK and U.S." 29 Nov. 2006. MMC. 26 Sep. 2008 <http://www.mmc.com/knowledgecenter/a_glynn_climate.pdf>.

clxxxiv Lifestyles of Health and Sustainability. 2008. 22 Sep. 2008 <http://www.lohas.com>.

clxxxv "What is LOHAS?" Sep. 2008. Sustainable Business Council. 28 Sep. 2008 <http://www.sustainablebc.org/v2/who_vendors.html>.

clxxxvi Bemporad, Raphael, and M. Baranowski. "Highlights from the BBMG Conscious Consumer Report: Conscious Consumers Are Changing the Rules of Marketing. Are You Ready?" Nov. 2007. BBMG. 22 Sep. 2008 <http://www.bbmg.com/pdfs/BBMG_Conscious_Consumer_White_Paper.pdf>.

clxxxvii Sass, Erik. "Advertisers: Teens Value Environment, Buy from Socially Responsible Companies." 20 March 2007. RelightNY. 22 Sep. 2008 <http://www.relightny.com/press/MediaDailyNews_RelightNY_3_22.pdf>.
clxxxviii Sass, Erik. "Advertisers: Teens Value Environment, Buy from Socially Responsible Companies." 20 March 2007. RelightNY. 22 Sep. 2008 <http://www.relightny.com/press/MediaDailyNews_RelightNY_3_22.pdf>.
clxxxix "Going Green." Sep. 2008. Yankelovich MONITOR Perspective. 22 Sep. 2008 <http://www.yankelovich.com/index.php?option=com_content&task=category&sectionid=13&id=75&Itemid=257>.
cxc "GoodPurpose." Sep. 2008. Edelman. 22 Sep. 2008 <http://www.goodpurposecommunity.com/>.

CHAPTER 12: CORPORATE SOCIAL RESPONSIBILITY REPORTING

cxci George Pohle and Jeff Hittner. "Attaining Sustainable Growth Through Corporate Social Responsibility." IBM Institute for Business Value Study. 12 Feb. 2008.
cxcii "SIRAN-KLD Study Shows Nearly Half of S&P 100 Index Companies Now Report on Environmental, Social, and Governance Issues." 25 April 2007. Siran.org. 28 Sep. 2008 <http://www.siran.org/SIRANPR20070427.pdf>.
cxciii Carbon Disclosure Project. "CDP5 FT 500 Report Summary." 23 Jan. 2008 <http://www.cdproject.net/cdp5reports.asp>.
cxciv "Assessing the Impact of Societal Issues: A McKinsey Global Survey." Sep. 2000. The McKinsey Quarterly. 22 Sep. 2008 <http://www.mckinseyquarterly.com/article_page.aspx?ar=2077&l2=7&l3=10>.
cxcv "SIRAN-KLD Study Shows Nearly Half of S&P 100 Index Companies Now Report on Environmental, Social, and Governance Issues." 25 April 2007. Siran.org. 28 Sep. 2008 <http://www.siran.org/SIRANPR20070427.pdf>.
cxcvi "What We Do." Dec. 2007. Global Reporting Initiative. 17 Dec. 2007 <http://www. globalreporting.org/AboutGRI/WhatWeDo/>.
cxcvii "Board Unanimously Approves the G3 Guidelines for Release." 25 July 2006. Global Reporting Initiative. 28 Aug. 2008 <http://www. globalreporting.org/NewsEventsPress/PressResources/PressRelease1.htm>.
cxcviii Ceres. 2007. 17 Dec. 2008 <www.ceres.org>.

^{cxcix} "Social Responsibility." 9 April 2008. ISO. 17 Dec. 2007 <www.iso.org/sr>.
^{cc} "Social Responsibility." 9 April 2008. ISO. 17 Dec. 2007 <www.iso.org/sr>.

CONCLUSION

^{cci} "Social Responsibility." 9 April 2008. ISO. 17 Dec. 2007 <www.iso.org/sr>.
^{cci} Climate Counts. 2008. 17 Dec. 2008 <http://www.climatecounts. org/index.php>.

GLOSSARY

^{ccii} Frosch, Robert A., and Nicholas E. Gallopoulos. "Strategies For Manufacturing." Scientific American 189.3 1989): 144-152.
^{cciii} Erkman, S. "Industrial Ecology: An Historical View." J. Cleaner Prod. 5.1-2 (1997): 1.
^{cciv} http://www.global100.org/2007/index.asp
^{ccv} http://money.cnn.com/magazines/fortune/bestcompanies/2007/index.html
^{ccvi} http://money.cnn.com/magazines/fortune/mostadmired/2007/index.html
^{ccvii} http://www.sustainability.com/insight/research-article.asp?id=865
^{ccviii} http://www.business-ethics.com/whats_new/100best.html
^{ccix} http://www.npicenter.com/anm/templates/newsATemp.aspx?articleid =18040&zoneid=2